Working toward Better Pay

A WORLD BANK STUDY

Working toward Better Pay
Earning Dynamics in Ghana and Tanzania

Paolo Falco, Andrew Kerr, Pierella Paci, and Bob Rijkers

THE WORLD BANK
Washington, D.C.

Contents

Boxes

Figures

Tables

Acknowledgments

We would like to thank the Centre for the Study of African Economies at Oxford University and in particular Francis Teal, Justin Sandefur, Andrew Zeitlin, and Simon Quinn for generously providing access to the data. We are grateful to Louise Cord, Louise Fox, John Giles, Mary Hallward-Driemeier, David McKenzie, David Newhouse, Emanuel Skoufias, Ana Revenga, and especially Francis Teal for useful comments and to the World Bank Gender Action Plan (GAP) Trust Fund for financial support. All errors are our own. The views expressed here are those of the authors and do not necessarily represent the views of the World Bank, its Executive Board, or member countries.

About the Authors

Paolo Falco is an ESRC postdoctoral fellow at the University of Oxford (Centre for the Study of African Economies). His research lies at the intersection of labour, behavioral, and experimental economics, with a focus on developing countries. He holds a PhD in economics from Oxford University and a BSc Economics degree from the University College London. He is a Junior Prize Fellow of the Royal Economics Society, and, in recent years, he has been a visiting scholar at the École Normale Supérieure (Paris School of Economics) and at the University of Copenhagen. His previous work experiences include collaborations with the World Bank, the International Monetary Fund, the Institute for Fiscal Studies, and the UK Independent Commission on Banking.

Andrew Kerr is a senior research officer at DataFirst, University of Cape Town. He studied economics and applied mathematics at the University of Kwa Zulu-Natal, South Africa, before completing the MPhil and DPhil in economics at Oxford between 2006 and 2011. His research interests include labor and transport economics. He previously worked as a consultant for the South African Competition Commission and the World Bank, and he helped manage household and firm surveys in Tanzania and Ghana for the Centre for the Study of Africa Economies.

Pierella Paci is lead economist in the Office of the Vice President of the Poverty Reduction and Economic Management Network (PREM). In her 15-year career at the World Bank, Ms. Paci has held technical, operational, and management positions in the Europe and Central Asia region, in the Gender and Development Group, and in the Poverty Reduction and Equity Group where she led the Employment and Migration Team and the Shock and Crisis thematic area. Prior to joining the World Bank Group, she was assistant professor of economics at the University of Sussex (UK) and associate professor of economics at City University, London. Ms. Paci holds a degree in economics from the University of Rome (Italy) and a PhD in economics from the Victoria University of Manchester (UK). She has written extensively in the areas of labor economics, gender economics, inequality and poverty, jobs, and human development.

Bob Rijkers is an economist in the Trade and International Integration Unit of the Development Economics Research Group in the World Bank Group. He is interested in political economy, trade, and labor market issues. Since joining the World Bank full time in 2008, he has worked in the Poverty Reduction Anchor of the PREM network, the Macroeconomics and Growth Unit of the Development Economics Research Group, and the Office of the Chief Economist of the Middle East and Northern Africa region. He holds a BA in science and social sciences from University College Utrecht, Utrecht University, and an MPhil and DPhil in economics from the University of Oxford.

Abbreviations

ASD	aggregate state dependence
CF	control function
FD	first difference
FE	fixed effect
GDP	gross domestic product
GSD	genuine state dependence
HBS	household budget survey
LIC	low-income country
MIC	middle-income country
ML	maximum likelihood
NGO	nongovernmental organization
OLS	ordinary least squares
RDG	reading
UPS	urban panel surveys
WG	within group

Executive Summary

This study uses the Ghana and Tanzania Urban Panel Surveys to examine the determinants of earnings, earnings growth, and low-pay/high-pay transitions in the high growth period 2004–08 and to identify communalities/differences across the two countries. The analysis highlights the importance of job characteristics in determining earnings and earnings growth.

On average, even after controlling for ability bias, returns to cognitive skills and education are higher in wage employment than in self-employment, with the civil service and large firms paying the highest wages. However, the high within-sector heterogeneity in earnings means that self-employment is not always inferior to wage employment.

Earnings growth is difficult to predict, and its drivers vary across sectors. Over the short horizons of this study, the sharpest changes in earnings were associated with job switches. These findings point toward path dependence in pay trajectories, and this conclusion is reinforced by the finding that being in low-paid employment has a *scarring* effect: it undermines future earnings prospects. Moreover, the determinants of *low-pay incidence* (that is, the risk of becoming low paid) differ from those of *low-pay persistence* (that is, the risk of remaining low paid). Women and young workers are especially likely to fall into, and remain trapped in, low-pay activities.

Although the data reviewed for this study cover 2004–08, recent developments in the economic situation and structure of the countries may have reinforced the messages that emerge from this analysis.

CHAPTER 1

Introduction

Improving access to productive employment is a key policy challenge, especially in low-income countries (LICs), where the only asset in abundance is labor. Since returns from working are the sole sources of income for these countries' citizens, changes in labor earnings are more important in explaining changes in per capita household income than changes in any other source of income (Fields et al. 2003a, 2003b). Thus, policies that increase labor earnings help accelerate poverty reduction and growth.

Individual workers can increase earnings by (i) working more hours; (ii) increasing labor productivity in a given job (if self-employed and/or if wages adjust to productivity); and (iii) moving to a job that offers higher returns per hours worked. Yet, the understanding of individual earnings dynamics remains limited (Fields 2008). A good deal of empirical literature has focused on identifying engines for, and barriers to, employment generation and, in particular, on the links between gross domestic product (GDP) growth and job creation. However, less attention has been paid to understanding the factors that lead to larger and faster pay increases, and when these factors are studied, the implicit assumption is often that they are the same as those that bring individuals out of low-pay employment. The small but growing body of literature points to strong persistence in earnings over time, but it remains unclear to what extent this persistence is due to individual heterogeneity rather than to the fact that being in a low-paying job itself undermines future earnings prospects.

Shortages of longitudinal data are often quoted as the main reason for the limited understanding of earnings dynamics and their determinants in the developing world. However, evidence from developed countries suggests that being in a low-paying job might have severe scarring effects (Cappellari and Jenkins 2004). Another relatively unexplored issue is the extent to which determinants of earnings vary across types of activities and sectors. For example, it is still unclear how the returns to skills vary across sectors and whether specific skills are valued differently in different sectors. Neither is it known whether the differences in returns to education between these types of activities reflect ability bias. Empirical evidence on the characteristics of successful entrepreneurs and how these might differ from those of wage workers also remains scarce, even though self-employment in microenterprises is an increasingly important source of income and employment in Africa (Fox and Gaal 2008) and other regions (International Labour Organization [ILO] 2002).

These knowledge gaps are of particular concern in LICs, where poverty is less likely to be the consequence of a lack of employment, but rather of limited access to high productivity, well-paid jobs (see, for example, Johansson de Silva and Paci [2012]). In this context, the main policy challenge is to identify barriers to productivity and wage growth, rather than only employment creation.

Building on ongoing research on earnings mobility, this study uses unusually rich longitudinal data from Ghana and Tanzania to identify engines of, and barriers to, earnings and earnings mobility. It examines the role of individual characteristics—such as gender, age, and skills—and characteristics of the job, but it also focuses on the role of job switches—for example, moves into and out of self-employment. It zooms in particularly on the drivers of transitions between low-paying and high-paying jobs, and addresses questions such as whether being low paid is a transitory or permanent phenomenon, and whether it has a scarring effect on an individual's employment prospects. The extent to which earnings dynamics differ for women and young adults is also discussed in detail.

Tanzania and Ghana provide a very relevant context in which to examine these issues. Tanzania's *National Strategy for Growth and the Reduction of Poverty* emphasizes the creation of productive employment opportunities to support poverty reduction, highlighting the potential of self-employment to provide viable earning opportunities. Promoting entrepreneurship is also an important pillar of Ghana's *Poverty Reduction and Growth Strategy II*. Job creation and enhancing returns to self-employment are progressively becoming more pressing policy issues, because both countries have experienced rapid growth in the proportion of the workforce that is self-employed outside agriculture. In particular, over recent years, as Ghana has become a middle-income country (MIC) and joined the club of oil producers, increasing access to productive employment for a growing part of the population has become an important pillar of the country's inclusive growth strategy.

Moreover, the cross-country comparison of earnings dynamics and labor market transitions helps shed light on the institutional factors that promote labor market mobility and entrepreneurship. The relevance of these results for policy making extends beyond these two countries. The structure of the Tanzanian and Ghanaian labor markets is typical of LICs, in which self-employment in small-scale activities accounts for a very large proportion of all employment (Kingdon, Sandefur, and Teal 2005). From a pragmatic point of view, the availability of unique, novel data sets (see chapter 3), which allow analysis of previously unexplored policy issues, makes these countries very appealing case studies.

This study next presents a brief review of related literature (chapter 2), followed by a descriptive overview of the labor markets in the two countries (chapter 3). The determinants of earnings *levels* are examined in chapter 4, and those of earnings *growth* in chapter 5. Chapter 6 focuses on low-pay/high-pay transitions and analyzes whether the experience of being in a low-paying job undermines an individual's future earnings prospects. Finally, chapter 7 discusses key policy implications.

CHAPTER 2

What Did We Know about the Determinants of Earnings and Earnings Growth in Ghana and Tanzania?

Empirical evidence suggests that the determinants of earnings and their growth in Ghana and Tanzania, as in other countries, depend not only on workers' human capital and gender but also on the location, sector, scale, and productivity of the workplace.

The Determinants of Earnings Levels

Several studies show that human capital is an important determinant of earnings in both Ghana and Tanzania. Söderbom et al. (2006) found returns to education in Tanzania of between 6 and 13 percent, based on data from manufacturing sector surveys. Pissarides (2002) found that the return to education in Tanzania was 10 percent when estimated using household survey data from 1991, and 4 percent based on enterprise survey data from the same year. These estimates are roughly in line with those for developed countries (Card 2001). Quinn and Teal (2008) also found the returns to education in Tanzania to be convex, that is, the marginal returns rise with educational attainment. These findings are in line with previous results for Ghana (Rankin, Sandefur, and Teal 2007) and with those from developed economies (Belzil and Hansen 2002).

These higher returns to education at higher levels of educational attainment may be driven by differences in activities and sectors rather than growth in earnings within given jobs, since better education is strongly correlated with higher probability of finding better-paid employment. Fafchamps, Söderbom, and Benhassine (2009), for example, found that more than 50 percent of the education-wage premia in manufacturing is accounted for by sectoral sorting. The estimated returns to education might also be driven by innate ability bias, due to more able individuals both acquiring more education and having better employment opportunities. However, separating the impact of innate ability from that of acquired education is rarely possible due to data limitations.

Gender also plays an important role. Women typically earn less than men, both in wage employment and self-employment. The majority of microenterprises in African countries are operated by women, despite female-headed firms being typically less profitable than others. This suggests that women lack alternative income-earning opportunities (Mead and Liedholm 1998).[1] Earnings generally also rise with age, and youth face difficulty finding high-paid employment, possibly due to lack of labor market experience and lack of financial capital to set up profitable enterprises.

Wages and their determinants—especially returns to skills—vary substantially both across and within sectors and across locations. Indeed, a striking feature of developing country labor markets is the heterogeneity in earnings for workers with similar observable characteristics. For example, public and private formal sector employees are typically better paid, enjoy more stable employment, and better benefits than self-employed and informal sector workers. Earnings also rise with firm size: Söderbom et al. (2006), for example, found a strong positive association between firm size and wages in both Ghana and Tanzania, even after controlling for worker characteristics. This result survives the application of fixed-effect estimation techniques to control for unobserved determinants of earnings that might also be driving sorting of workers into larger firms. Using data from manufacturing firms in 10 countries, Fafchamps and Söderbom (2006) show that the positive correlation between firm size and wages is consistent with efficiency wage models based on moral hazard with costly supervision.

The existence of pay differentials and differential rates of earnings growth for workers with similar observable characteristics across and within sectors in firms of different size may be indicative of labor market segmentation, or could reflect differences in unobserved skills or compensating differentials. Rankin, Sandefur, and Teal (2007) argue that the large wage differentials observed in Ghana for comparable workers across different sectors represent compelling evidence of existing labor market rigidities that keep wages above market-clearing level and lead to segmentation.[2] Evidence from Latin America suggests that self-employment in small enterprises is largely a voluntary phenomenon (Maloney 1999). However, the extent to which these findings can be generalized to Africa, where countries are poorer and inequality lower remains questionable.

The Determinants of Earnings Growth

While the determinants of earnings *levels* have been the subject of a voluminous body of research, the determinants of earnings *growth* have received far less attention. Fields et al. (2003a, 2003b), using household data from Indonesia, South Africa, Spain, and Venezuela, found that job changes are the most important factor behind earnings growth and that the roles of age and education are surprisingly weak. Similarly, Quinn and Teal (2008) found that education and age are not significantly correlated with earnings growth in Tanzania, and earnings rise more quickly for those with low levels of education. These findings raise the question of whether acquisition of *any* skills leads to faster earnings growth, or whether specific skills are rewarded differently across sectors.

Evidence on Low-Pay Persistence and Scarring

Evidence from developed countries suggests also that being in a low-paying job has a negative effect on earnings prospects, a phenomenon referred to as labor market *scarring*.[3] However, it is not clear to what extent these findings can be generalized to the less rigid labor markets of the developing world.

Notes

1. Tanzania seems to deviate from this general pattern since most microenterprises in that country are operated by men.

2. For a more extensive overview of potential causes of sector differences, see Kingdon, Sandefur, and Teal (2005).

3. See for example, Cappellari and Jenkins (2004), Cappellari (2002), and Stewart and Swaffield (1999).

CHAPTER 3

Data and Descriptive Statistics

Ghana and Tanzania Urban Panel Surveys

The Ghana and Tanzania Urban Panel Surveys (UPS) were designed by the Centre for the Study of African Economies at the University of Oxford to track the labor market experience of a representative sample of urban working-age individuals (ages 15–65) over several years. In both countries, surveys began in 2004 and respondents were subsequently visited at yearly intervals for three years in Tanzania (2004–06) and five years in Ghana (2004–08). The 2007 wave in Ghana, however, was obtained from recall questions administered during the 2008 survey, and this may have undermined its comparability with the other waves. The results presented in this study are robust to excluding 2007.

The Ghana survey covers a stratified random sample of urban households from the 2000 census. In Tanzania, the sample was drawn from the households visited by the 2000–01 Household Budget Survey (HBS), conducted by the Tanzania Bureau of National Statistics, with additional randomly selected households added in 2006.[1]

The surveys have a number of strengths. In addition to the longitudinal dimension, the fact that the UPS were designed to record the net earnings of both wage earners and the self-employed is an obvious advantage, because it enables comparisons between these two categories. The strong comparability of the two surveys also facilitates comparisons across countries. In addition, in 2005 and 2006, respondents undertook several tests specifically designed to measure their mathematical and verbal skills and their noncognitive abilities. This detailed and relatively uncommon information makes it possible to separate the impact of innate intelligence, acquired skills, and education on earnings levels and dynamics.

However, a drawback of the data is the relatively high attrition rate, especially in Tanzania. Table 3.1 presents the percentages of respondents interviewed in the first year (2004) who were interviewed again in any of the following years. However, the model predicting attrition suggests that attrition is largely random, and therefore not a strong concern from an econometric point of view.[2]

Table 3.1 Panel Retention Rates

Country	2005	2006	2008
Ghana	0.79	0.63	0.40
Tanzania	0.75	0.45	—

Source: World Bank; values arrived at using the Tanzanian and Ghanaian UPSs.
Note: — = not available.

Another potential limitation is the fact that the data cover only the period up to 2008. Since then, both countries have continued to enjoy rapid growth, and Ghana recently joined the middle-income category and the oil producers' club.

Construction of Key Explanatory Variables

This section discusses only the most important variables. For an overview of other variables used in the analysis, see appendix A.

Earnings. Earnings are defined as pretax monthly earnings. For wage workers, they include average bonuses and allowances received in any given month. For the self-employed, they are proxied by a measure of monthly profits obtained after guiding them through the concepts of business revenues and costs. Thus, while the earnings of wage workers purely capture the returns to labor, the earnings of the self-employed may also reflect returns to capital as well as the contributions of unpaid workers (who may be members of the same household). Since only 19 percent of the self-employed report hiring any paid or unpaid workers in both countries, the latter issue is likely to be of second-order magnitude and the regression analysis partially corrects for this bias by controlling for the total number of employees.

Occupational Categories. Paid workers are divided into three main categories: (i) self-employed entrepreneurs (with or without employees), (ii) wage earners in private firms, and (iii) civil servants.[3] All respondents *not employed for pay* fall into a residual category of unpaid workers. This includes students, unpaid family workers, unpaid apprentices, working-age individuals who are temporarily or permanently out of the labor force, and unemployed job seekers.

Skills Variables. The survey includes four ability tests: a mathematics test, a language comprehension test, a reading ability test, and the Raven's Matrices, which are designed to measure the cognitive and noncognitive abilities of the respondent. In this study, the term "cognitive skills" refers to those skills that are developed or improved through schooling and education—that is, literacy and ability to perform mathematical calculations. Noncognitive skills, on the other hand, are considered either innate—that is, genetically inherited—or the product of early development.

The mathematics test was a combination of practical problems (such as computing the duration of a trip, given distance and speed) and general arithmetic. The language comprehension test required respondents to read a short text and answer questions related to its contents, and the reading test required respondents to read aloud a series of words and an entire sentence, and translate a series of English words into their native language. The non-cognitive skills Raven's Matrices required the respondent to understand the pattern linking several objects within a matrix by simple intuition and logic, and complete the matrix accordingly. Points were awarded for fluency of reading and correct translations. The math and language comprehension tests were administered both in 2005 and 2006, but, despite maintaining comparable structure and contents, they were changed between 2005 and 2006. The reading ability and Raven's Matrices were added in 2006. For comparability's sake and to retain the maximum sample size, the scores of respondents who took the test in both waves were averaged so that the skills captured by such tests are time invariant over the relatively short time frame covered by the surveys.

Table 3.2 shows pairwise correlations between skills proxies and years in formal education. With the exception of two cases in Tanzania, all correlations between scores are positive, but those between the math and the language comprehension scores are much higher in both Ghana and Tanzania than the correlation between the Raven's score and linguistic abilities. This provides empirical support for the assumption that both math and literacy skills are functions of schooling, while noncognitive skills (proxied by the

Table 3.2 Correlation Coefficients between Skills Proxies

	Ghana				
	Language comprehension	*Math*	*Reading*	*Raven's Matrices*	*Education*
Language comprehension	1				
Math	0.66	1			
Reading	0.33	0.51	1		
Raven's Matrices	0.37	0.478	0.29	1	
Education	0.37	0.44	0.53	0.19	1

Source: World Bank; values arrived at using the Tanzanian and Ghanaian UPSs.

	Tanzania				
	Language comprehension	*Math*	*Reading*	*Raven's Matrices*	*Education*
Language comprehension	1				
Math	0.65	1			
Reading	0.36	0.27	1		
Raven's Matrices	0.19	0.25	0.11	1	
Education	−0.01	−0.03	0.52	0.33	1

Source: World Bank; values arrived at using the Tanzanian and Ghanaian UPSs.

Raven's score) are innate. The hypothesis is also supported by the fact that formal education in Ghana is highly correlated with literacy (particularly reading abilities) and math skills, but only weakly correlated with innate ability (Raven's). In Tanzania, the correlations between scores in language comprehension and math and the years in school are negative, but very close to zero and insignificant, while the correlation between education and reading abilities is stronger. What accounts for these differences across countries is not clear.

Descriptive Statistics

Occupational Categories

Figure 3.1 presents the pooled data on the percentage of workers in different occupations from all survey waves. The self-employed are by far the largest group, and wage employment covers approximately 25 percent of the sample in both countries. However, at nearly one-third of wage employment, the public sector accounts for a considerably larger share of employment in Tanzania than in Ghana. In both countries, close to one quarter of the working-age population is either unemployed or out of the labor force and public sector employees have the highest average educational attainment followed by private sector wage workers (figure 3.2). The self-employed have the lowest average levels of formal education, even lower than the average education levels of those who are not working.

Mean Earnings by Occupation

As shown in figures 3.3a and 3.3b, in both countries, mean earnings are highest in the public sector and in large private enterprises and lowest for entrepreneurs without employees and wage earners in small firms.[4]

Figure 3.1 Occupational Categories

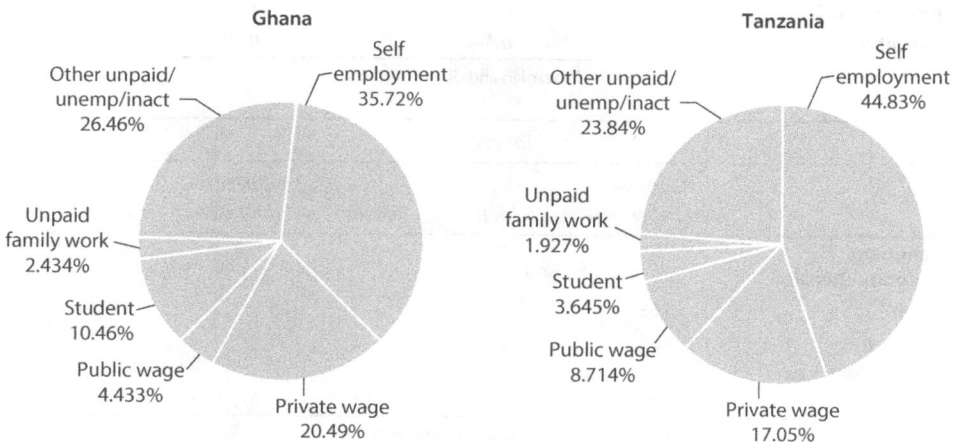

Ghana

Other unpaid/unemp/inact 26.46%
Self employment 35.72%
Unpaid family work 2.434%
Student 10.46%
Public wage 4.433%
Private wage 20.49%

Tanzania

Other unpaid/unemp/inact 23.84%
Self employment 44.83%
Unpaid family work 1.927%
Student 3.645%
Public wage 8.714%
Private wage 17.05%

Source: World Bank; values arrived at using the Tanzanian and Ghanaian UPSs.

Figure 3.2 Average Education by Occupation

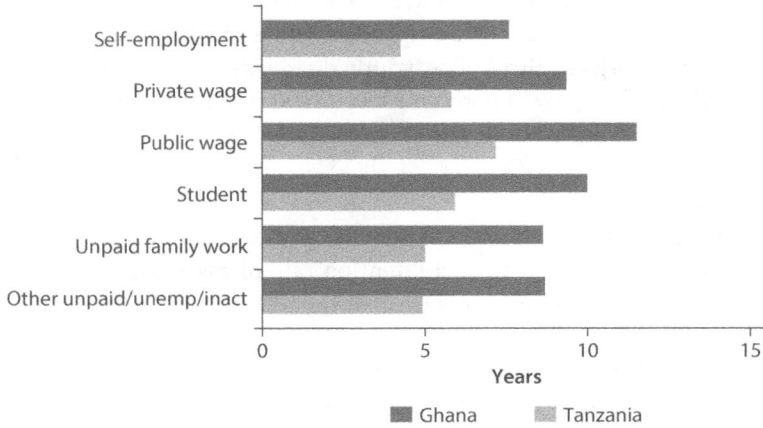

Source: World Bank; values arrived at using the Tanzanian and Ghanaian UPSs.

Figure 3.3a Mean Earnings by Occupation (Ghana)

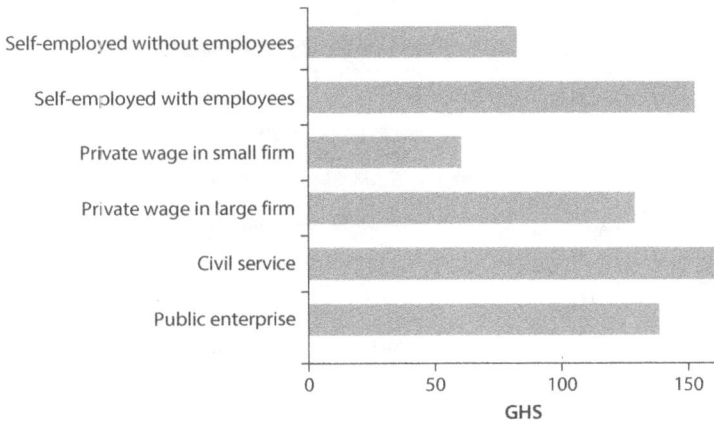

Figure 3.3b Mean Earnings by Occupation (Tanzania)

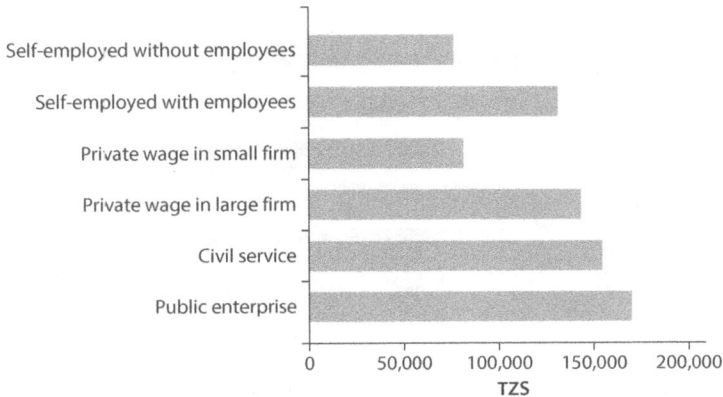

Source: World Bank; values arrived at using the Tanzanian and Ghanaian UPSs.
Note: GHS = Ghana cedis; TZS = Tanzanian shillings.

Figures 3.4a, 3.4b, 3.5a, and 3.5b show the existence of a significant wage disadvantage for women and workers under age 30 in every sector. In Ghana, the gender gap is largest among the self-employed, while in Tanzania, it is most pronounced in small private firms. The youth disadvantage in Ghana is most striking among the self-employed with employees and small firm workers, while in Tanzania it is most striking in the public sector.

Sector Transitions

Table 3.3 shows that the most persistent occupational category over a one-year period is self-employment, which has a retention rate of more than 80 percent in both countries. Overall, the percentage of workers who move between occupations is surprisingly high. The self-employed and the private wage workers display similar rates of transition out of paid employment (11 to 14 percent), and the rate is only marginally lower for public sector employees (10 percent for

Figure 3.4a Mean Earnings by Occupation and Gender (Ghana)

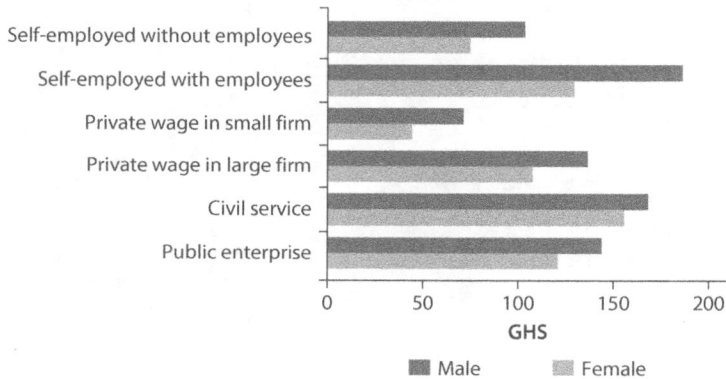

Figure 3.4b Mean Earnings by Occupation and Gender (Tanzania)

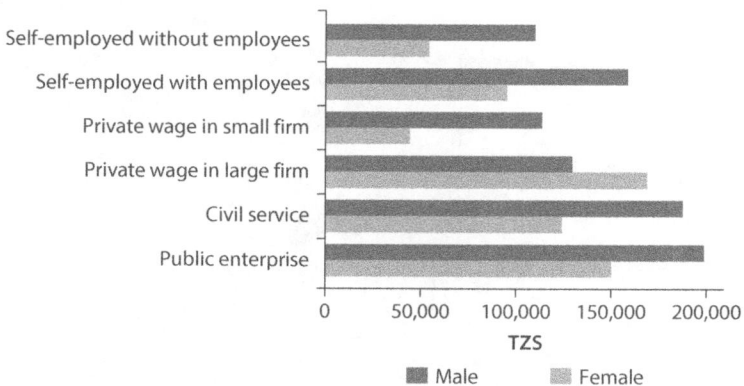

Source: World Bank; values arrived at using the Tanzanian and Ghanaian UPSs.

Figure 3.5a Mean Earnings by Occupation and Age (Ghana)

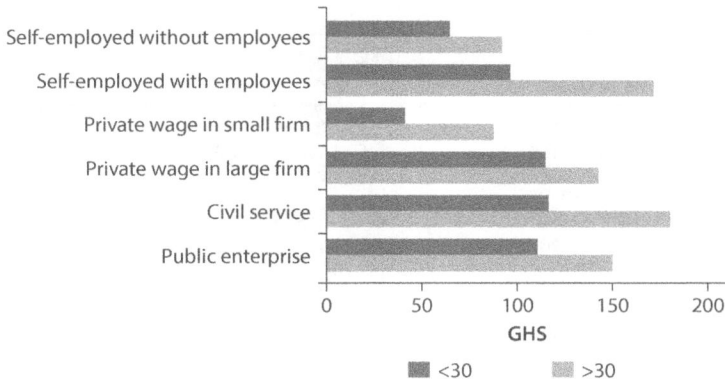

Figure 3.5b Mean Earnings by Occupation and Age (Tanzania)

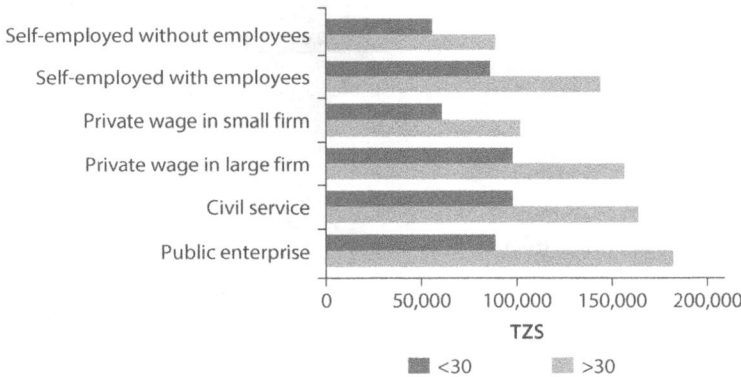

Source: World Bank; values arrived at using the Tanzanian and Ghanaian UPSs.

Ghana and 11 percent for Tanzania). Transitions *into* paid employment, on the other hand, lead predominantly to self-employment in Tanzania (27 percent), but are equally distributed between self-employment and private wage employment in Ghana (12 percent for both).[5]

As expected, mobility is considerably higher over a two-year horizon. As table 3.4 shows, only 69 percent of the self-employed and 51 percent of public employees in Ghana—and 61 and 45 percent, respectively, in Tanzania—retained their jobs. Perhaps even more surprisingly, more than 25 percent of public employees (29 and 27 percent for Ghana and Tanzania, respectively) moved to the private sector within the two-year horizon, and 65 percent of the unpaid moved into paid employment in Tanzania, although only 43 percent did so in Ghana.

Finally, transitions over four years, presented in table 3.5 for Ghana, show a further reduction in the retention rates with the strongest flows being those

Table 3.3 One-Year Transitions between Occupations

	Ghana						Tanzania				
	Self	Priv wage	Pub wage	Unpaid	Total		Self	Priv wage	Pub wage	Unpaid	Total
Self	1,193	103	4	163	1,463	Self	414	23	10	69	516
	81.54	7.04	0.27	11.14	100		80.23	4.46	1.94	13.37	100
Priv wage	87	568	25	109	789	Priv wage	8	89	48	24	169
	11.03	71.99	3.17	13.81	100		4.73	52.66	28.4	14.2	100
Pub wage	7	26	117	17	167	Pub wage	3	17	45	8	73
	4.19	15.57	70.06	10.18	100		4.11	23.29	61.64	10.96	100
Unpaid	184	180	22	1,138	1,524	Unpaid	26	10	3	59	98
	12.07	11.81	1.44	74.67	100		26.53	10.2	3.06	60.2	100
Total	1,471	877	168	1,427	3,943	Total	451	139	106	160	856
	37.31	22.24	4.26	36.19	100		52.69	16.24	12.38	18.69	100

Source: World Bank; values arrived at using the Tanzanian and Ghanaian UPSs.
Notes: Self is self-employment, Priv wage is private wage employment, Pub wage is public wage employment, Unpaid is an unpaid family worker.

Table 3.4 Two-Year Transitions between Occupations

	Ghana						Tanzania				
	Self	Priv wage	Pub wage	Unpaid	Total		Self	Priv wage	Pub wage	Unpaid	Total
Self	642	120	7	157	926	Self	127	22	9	51	209
	69.33	12.96	0.76	16.95	100		60.77	10.53	4.31	24.4	100
Priv wage	79	265	19	109	472	Priv wage	7	33	34	18	92
	16.74	56.14	4.03	23.09	100		7.61	35.87	36.96	19.57	100
Pub wage	7	28	49	12	96	Pub wage	2	3	5	1	11
	7.29	29.17	51.04	12.5	100		18.18	27.27	45.45	9.09	100
Unpaid	184	177	27	510	898	Unpaid	6	4	3	7	20
	20.49	19.71	3.01	56.79	100		30	20	15	35	100
Total	912	590	102	788	2,392	Total	142	62	51	77	332
	38.13	24.67	4.26	32.94	100		42.77	18.67	15.36	23.19	100

Source: World Bank; values arrived at using the Tanzanian and Ghanaian UPSs.
Notes: Self is self-employment, Priv wage is private wage employment, Pub wage is public wage employment, Unpaid is an unpaid family worker.

Table 3.5 Four-Year Transitions between Occupations (Ghana)

	Self	Priv wage	Pub wage	Unpaid	Total
			Ghana		
Self	144	39	4	59	246
	58.54	15.85	1.63	23.98	100
Priv wage	17	37	7	18	79
	21.52	46.84	8.86	22.78	100
Pub wage	3	7	7	5	22
	13.64	31.82	31.82	22.73	100
Unpaid	50	50	7	83	190
	26.32	26.32	3.68	43.68	100
Total	214	133	25	165	537
	39.85	24.77	4.66	30.73	100

Source: World Bank; values arrived at using the Tanzanian and Ghanaian UPSs.
Notes: Self is self-employment, Priv wage is private wage employment, Pub wage is public wage employment, Unpaid is an unpaid family worker.

in/out of paid employment. At 32 percent, the flows into private wage employment from public sector employment are double those from self-employment.

Figure 3.6a and 3.6b report the changes in average earnings associated with different transitions in the two countries. Though it is impossible to draw conclusions on the relative financial gains associated with different transitions by simply looking at these figures, it is noticeable that transitions are generally associated with real earnings gains, both in *absolute* terms and *relative* to those who stay in a given occupation. For example, on average, the few workers who move from self-employment to a private sector wage job experience higher earnings growth than those who remain self-employed. Interestingly, however, transitions in the opposite direction also lead to higher earnings.

Earnings Growth

Figure 3.7 shows average one-year earnings growth in different occupations over 2004–08 for Ghana, and 2004–06 for Tanzania. On average, the earnings of the self-employed have grown faster than wages. The caveat with this finding, however, is that measurement error and transitory earnings shocks are both more prominent among the self-employed and therefore might have had an impact. Moreover, in Ghana, wages have grown relatively faster in the private sector than in the public sector, while this difference is negligible in Tanzania.

Figure 3.6a Average Earning Changes (%) by Type of Transition (Ghana)

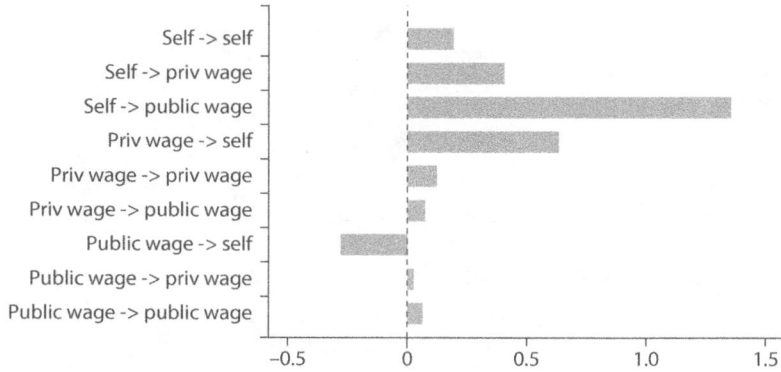

Figure 3.6b Average Earning Changes (%) by Type of Transition (Tanzania)

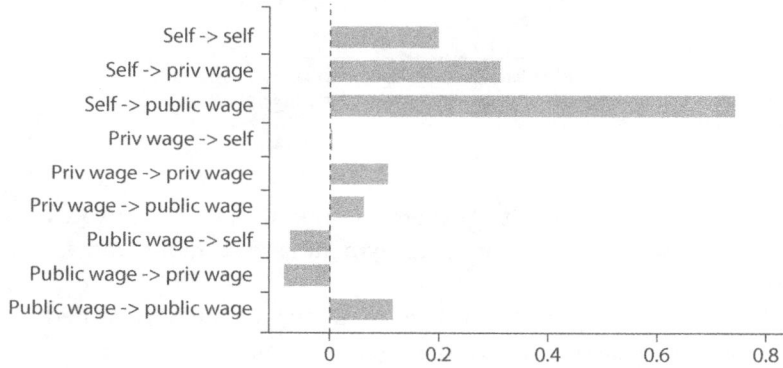

Source: World Bank; values arrived at using the Tanzanian and Ghanaian UPSs.
Notes: Self is self-employment, Priv wage is private wage employment, Pub wage is public wage employment.

Figure 3.7 One-Year Earnings Growth

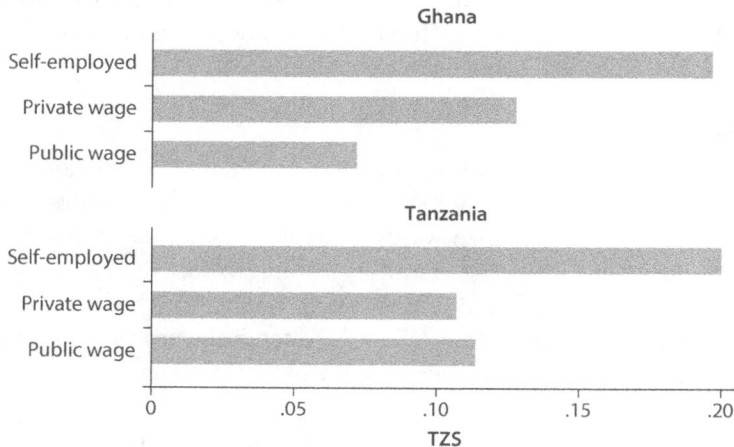

Source: World Bank; values arrived at using the Tanzanian and Ghanaian UPSs.

Table 3.6 One-Year Transitions from Low to High Pay

	Pay status at time t			
Pay status at time t-1	Low	High	Low	High
Country	Tanzania		Ghana	
Low	55.22	44.78	54.29	45.71
High	12.86	87.14	15.22	84.78

Source: World Bank; values arrived at using the Tanzanian and Ghanaian UPSs.

Low-pay/High-pay Transitions

In both countries, over 25 percent of paid workers are low paid (29 percent in Tanzania and 27 percent in Ghana).[6] However, table 3.6 shows this to be mostly a transitory state in both countries as nearly half of the low-paid move to high-pay occupations within the two years covered by the analysis. In addition, upward mobility is considerably higher than downward mobility: only 15 percent (or less) of the high-paid workers falls into low pay during this period.

Notes

1. For more information on the sampling strategy, visit http://www.csae.ox.ac.uk/datasets/Ghana-Tanz-UHPS/default.html.

2. The analysis also attempted to correct for attrition bias using the inverse probability weighting method proposed by Moffit, Fitzgerald, and Gottschalk (1999). The results (available from the authors), suggest that the qualitative pattern of results is robust to correcting attrition bias, though individual coefficient estimates occasionally changed.

3. Civil servants are defined as those working for the government, international organizations, or nongovernmental organizations (NGOs) and employees in state-owned enterprises. NGOs workers are categorized as civil sector employees since they are likely to benefit from higher wages and to face a wage-setting structure that is more akin to that prevailing in the civil service sector than that operating in the private sector.

4. Small firms are defined as firms with less than 10 employees.

5. High mobility might reflect measurement error; however, over longer time horizons, measurement error ought to be less of a concern as the signal-to-noise ratio in the data should increase. In other words, over longer horizons, a smaller share of the transitions will be due to measurement error instead of genuine switching.

6. A worker/job is defined as *low paid* if s/he/it earns/pays less than US$1.25 a day. This is in line with the US$1.25 a day poverty line defined by Chen and Ravallion (2008). However, it is important to note that, contrary to typical poverty analyses, the focus here is on low pay rather that poverty. Thus, the low-pay line is defined in terms of individual earnings rather than equivalized household consumption; thus, the low-earnings threshold is conservative.

CHAPTER 4

The Determinants of Earnings Levels

In this chapter we explore the determinants of earnings levels using the Tanzanian and Ghanaian Urban Panel Surveys. We explore the extent to which human capital determines earnings, as well as the challenges faced by women and young people in employment. We also discuss other determinants of earnings and whether these determinants differ by sector. See box 4.1 for the key hypotheses we test in this chapter and a summary of its main results.

Framework and Baseline Specification

The starting point of the analysis is a semilogarithmic Mincerian earnings equation, where the log of monthly earnings is modeled as function of the respondent's gender; height; age and age squared (to allow for nonlinear effects of age on earnings); a self-reported measure of tenure; the log of hours worked; years of schooling and its square (to allow for nonlinear effect of education); firm size; a dummy indicating whether the respondent has ever completed an apprenticeship; and sector, city, and year dummies.

The results of a simple ordinary least squares (OLS) regression are presented in columns 1 (Ghana) and 5 (Tanzania) of table 4.1. A number of patterns are qualitatively similar across countries:

- *Earnings rise with age and experience.* Age-earnings profiles are *concave*: earnings rise quickly with age, but the increase declines as workers grow older, and eventually becomes negative. At age 42 in Tanzania and 43 in Ghana, the turning point is remarkably similar in the two countries. Even after controlling for age, self-reported tenure is associated with significantly higher earnings levels in Ghana, but the estimated association is insignificant in Tanzania. This positive correlation between tenure and earnings may reflect the accumulation of job-specific human capital or the fact that better matches between workers and firms are more likely to survive.
- *They also raise with firm size.* The association between firm size and earnings is especially pronounced for entrepreneurs, potentially reflecting returns to

---

Box 4.1 Key Hypotheses and Main Findings

Hypothesis 1: Education and skills play a crucial role in determining earnings.
Main finding: The marginal returns to education are high and increase with the level of educational attainment.
- The estimated returns to education are robust to controlling for ability bias.
- Cognitive skills are significant predictors of earnings.
- Apprentices are either unpaid or paid significantly less than other workers.
- Apprenticeships do not lead to higher earnings.

Hypothesis 2: Women and youth face special challenges.
Main finding: Women/youth earn systematically less than men/older workers and have different returns to education.
- The gender differential is *highest* among the self-employed and *lowest* in the public sector.
- Women's earnings grow slower with age and reach a peak later in life than those of men.
- Women experience positive returns to primary education, while men only benefit from postprimary education.
- Returns to education are higher and more highly convex among youth.

Hypothesis 3: The determinants of earnings vary by sector.
Main finding: The key factors determining earnings vary substantially across sectors and across firms.
- The returns to education and cognitive skills are highest in wage employment.
- Large firms pay workers with same observable characteristics more than small firms do

---

capital. However, this could also be interpreted as evidence of the existence of a wedge between productivity and wages paid by large enterprises.
- *Men tend to earn more than women,* even after controlling for educational attainment, other observable characteristics, and job type. The gender gap is higher in Tanzania than in Ghana.

Education Pays, and Pays More and More

The coefficients on education presented in columns 1 and 5 in table 4.1 suggest that education and skills are associated with increased earnings and that the impact rises with the level of education, that is, the returns to education are *convex.*

Furthermore, acquired skills appear more important in determining earnings than innate ability. A common concern when estimating the returns to education is that more able individuals have higher potential wages, but are also likely to obtain more education and this leads to spurious high estimates of the returns to schooling. To control for this potential bias, the analysis initially uses a conventional control function (CF) approach, which includes the residuals of a model of educational attainment that uses distance to school as an exclusion restriction.

Table 4.1 Earnings Functions (OLS)

Dependent variable: log of monthly earnings	Ghana				Tanzania			
	OLS	CF— education	CF— education + apprentice	OLS with ability	OLS	CF— education	CF— education + apprentice	OLS with ability
Male	0.240***	0.163	0.161	0.203***	0.334***	0.318***	0.309***	0.329***
	(0.049)	(0.108)	(0.108)	(0.050)	(0.054)	(0.056)	(0.061)	(0.054)
Age	0.075***	0.061***	0.061***	0.078***	0.044***	0.037**	0.048	0.042***
	(0.014)	(0.023)	(0.023)	(0.014)	(0.016)	(0.018)	(0.034)	(0.016)
(age^2)/100	−0.089***	−0.069**	−0.069**	−0.093***	−0.045**	−0.032	−0.042	−0.041**
	(0.019)	(0.032)	(0.032)	(0.018)	(0.020)	(0.024)	(0.038)	(0.020)
Height (cm)	0.005	0.005	0.005	0.006	0.004	0.003	0.003	0.003
	(0.004)	(0.004)	(0.004)	(0.004)	(0.004)	(0.004)	(0.004)	(0.004)
Years in formal education	−0.040**	0.008	0.006	−0.037**	−0.056***	0.007	0.023	−0.053***
	(0.019)	(0.065)	(0.065)	(0.019)	(0.020)	(0.069)	(0.074)	(0.020)
(educ^2)/100	0.004***	0.004***	0.004***	0.004***	0.007***	0.007***	0.007***	0.007***
	(0.001)	(0.001)	(0.001)	(0.001)	(0.002)	(0.002)	(0.002)	(0.002)
Apprentice (currently)	−0.786***	−0.785***	−0.765***	−0.749***				
	(0.088)	(0.088)	(0.134)	(0.087)				
Apprenticeship completed	−0.039	−0.041	−0.010	−0.031	0.023	0.018	−0.072	0.021
	(0.049)	(0.050)	(0.132)	(0.049)	(0.094)	(0.095)	(0.261)	(0.095)
Ln (hours)	0.223***	0.225***	0.224***	0.217***	0.073	0.079	0.078	0.077
	(0.061)	(0.061)	(0.061)	(0.061)	(0.085)	(0.085)	(0.085)	(0.084)
Tenure, self–reported	0.013***	0.013***	0.013***	0.013***	0.006	0.006	0.006	0.006
	(0.003)	(0.003)	(0.003)	(0.003)	(0.004)	(0.004)	(0.004)	(0.004)
Ln (employees)	0.296***	0.296***	0.296***	0.289***	0.484***	0.487***	0.486***	0.471***
	(0.060)	(0.061)	(0.061)	(0.061)	(0.078)	(0.078)	(0.078)	(0.079)
Ln (firm size)	0.171***	0.171***	0.172***	0.160***	0.137***	0.136***	0.136***	0.132***
	(0.019)	(0.019)	(0.019)	(0.019)	(0.022)	(0.022)	(0.022)	(0.022)
Private wage	−0.256***	−0.257***	−0.258***	−0.252***	−0.056	−0.055	−0.053	−0.049
	(0.065)	(0.065)	(0.065)	(0.065)	(0.084)	(0.084)	(0.084)	(0.083)
Civil servant	0.566***	0.564***	0.564***	0.503***	0.474***	0.474***	0.476***	0.450***
	(0.087)	(0.087)	(0.087)	(0.086)	(0.087)	(0.087)	(0.088)	(0.088)
Public enterprise	−0.161	−0.158	−0.159	−0.175	0.269**	0.270**	0.273**	0.247**
	(0.119)	(0.120)	(0.120)	(0.119)	(0.128)	(0.128)	(0.128)	(0.125)
Residual education		−0.047	−0.046			−0.064	−0.080	
		(0.061)	(0.061)			(0.068)	(0.074)	
Residual apprenticeship			−0.032				0.092	
			(0.129)				(0.252)	
Math score				0.004***				0.003**
				(0.001)				(0.002)
City and year dummies	Yes	Yes	Yes	Yes	Yes	Yes	Yes	Yes

table continues next page

Table 4.1 Earnings Functions (OLS) *(continued)*

Dependent variable: log of monthly earnings	Ghana				Tanzania			
	OLS	CF— education	CF— education + apprentice	OLS with ability	OLS	CF— education	CF— education + apprentice	OLS with ability
Constant	−1.158*	−1.296**	−1.270*	−1.308**	8.586***	8.395***	7.928***	8.471***
	(0.639)	(0.649)	(0.658)	(0.632)	(0.697)	(0.717)	(1.442)	(0.694)
Number of observations	2,610	2,610	2,610	2,610	1,328	1,328	1,328	1,328
R^2	0.310	0.310	0.310	0.316	0.304	0.305	0.305	0.308
Adjusted R^2	0.304	0.304	0.304	0.310	0.293	0.293	0.293	0.297

Source: World Bank; values arrived at using the Tanzanian and Ghanaian UPSs.
Note: Standard errors are in parenthesis. CF= control function; OLS = ordinary least squares.
***$p<0.01$ **$p<0.05$ *$p<0.1$

However, as discussed in appendix B, the control function approach relies on rather restrictive assumptions, as well as on being able to successfully predict educational attainment. Thus, it is better to adopt a more direct methodology by adding to the equation an explanatory variable for individual ability proxied by performance on mathematics, English, reading, and Raven's tests.[1]

The impact of ability bias on the education results appears to be minimal. As shown in columns 2 and 5 of table 4.1, the residual of the model that uses the CF approach to predict educational attainment is never significant. The estimated returns to education do not change when the residual is included and, when they do, they become more positive, suggesting an upward rather than downward bias. The third specification—presented in columns 3 and 6—also includes a residual of a model that predicts the probability of being an apprentice and again is not significant. However, the estimated coefficient on doing an apprenticeship rises substantially, perhaps indicating that less able individuals sort into apprenticeships, as suggested by Kahyarara and Teal (2008).

The estimated returns to education are robust to including proxies for unobserved skills. Columns 4 and 8 show that the inclusion of an indicator of mathematical ability does not significantly affect returns to education. Other measures of ability are not included because mathematical ability is highly correlated with other skills (see table 3.2) and inclusion of the other proxies excessively reduces the sample size (see chapter 3). For purposes of comparability, the results of using different ability proxies are presented in table 4.2. The only indicators of ability that have a statistically significant positive impact on earnings when entered individually are the Raven's and English score in Ghana and the English and reading scores in Tanzania. When entered jointly, the proxies tend to lose their individual significance and show the "wrong" sign, presumably because they are highly correlated and the samples are small, especially in Tanzania. However, the ability proxies remain jointly significant in Ghana. More importantly, the inclusion of the proxies does not significantly affect the

Table 4.2 Earnings Functions—Controlling for Ability (OLS)

Dependent variable: log of monthly earnings	Ghana					Tanzania				
	(1)	(2)	(3)	(4)	(5)	(1)	(2)	(3)	(4)	(5)
Math score	0.004**	0.004***				0.001	0.003*			
	(0.002)	(0.001)				(0.002)	(0.001)			
Raven's score	0.002		0.003***			−0.002		−0.002		
	(0.001)		(0.001)			(0.002)		(0.002)		
English score	0.002			0.001**		0.002*			0.003**	
	(0.001)			(0.001)		(0.001)			(0.001)	
RDG score	−0.003**				0.000	0.001				0.004***
	(0.001)				(0.001)	(0.002)				(0.001)
Years in formal education	−0.053*	−0.044**	−0.041*	−0.046***	−0.068***	−0.059	−0.057***	0.004	−0.042	−0.055***
	(0.028)	(0.018)	(0.022)	(0.017)	(0.020)	(0.036)	(0.020)	(0.030)	(0.034)	(0.020)
(educ^2)/100	0.438**	0.412***	0.440***	0.465***	0.570***	0.735***	0.754***	0.441**	0.622***	0.739***
	(0.170)	(0.124)	(0.145)	(0.122)	(0.131)	(0.222)	(0.157)	(0.199)	(0.209)	(0.161)
Apprentice (currently)	−0.771***	−0.758***	−0.765***	−0.788***	−0.819***					
	(0.105)	(0.088)	(0.095)	(0.083)	(0.095)					
Have you ever been an apprentice?	−0.027	−0.021	0.008	−0.037	−0.063	0.099	0.020	0.103	0.079	0.030
	(0.062)	(0.049)	(0.056)	(0.048)	(0.054)	(0.090)	(0.091)	(0.089)	(0.089)	(0.092)
Controls	Yes	Yes	Yes	Yes	Yes	Yes	Yes	Yes	Yes	Yes
Number of observations	1,663	2,736	2,086	2,853	2,236	1,031	1,394	1,082	1,051	1,363
R^2	0.338	0.313	0.309	0.294	0.309	0.338	0.312	0.330	0.333	0.318
Adjusted R^2	0.328	0.307	0.301	0.288	0.302	0.321	0.300	0.316	0.318	0.306

Source: World Bank; values arrived at using the Tanzanian and Ghanaian UPSs.
Note: Controls included but not presented to conserve space: age, age squared, tenure, hours worked, firm size, sector, year dummies, city dummies. Standard errors are in parenthesis. OLS = ordinary least squares; RDG = Reading.
***$p<0.01$ **$p<0.05$ *$p<0.1$

estimated returns to education or to doing an apprenticeship. The estimated returns to education are also robust to controlling for Raven's test scores, which, arguably, is a relatively clean proxy for innate ability.

Special Challenges for Youth and Women

As shown in table 4.3, differences in the determinants of earnings emerge between men and women, and between younger and older workers:[2]

- *Gender gaps in earnings exist in all sectors.* The gap is *highest* among the self-employed and *lowest* in the public sector. To the extent that this is driven by discrimination, the public sector appears to be a more gender-sensitive employer.

Table 4.3 Earnings Functions by Age and Gender

Dependent variable: log of monthly earnings	Ghana				Tanzania			
	Women	Men	Young	Old	Women	Men	Young	Old
Male			0.172**	0.222***			0.182**	0.358***
			(0.068)	(0.071)			(0.092)	(0.062)
Age	0.064***	0.098***	0.037***	−0.000	0.024	0.069***	0.046***	0.003
	(0.022)	(0.017)	(0.010)	(0.004)	(0.022)	(0.022)	(0.015)	(0.004)
(age^2)/100	−0.069**	−0.121***			−0.025	−0.071**		
	(0.029)	(0.023)			(0.028)	(0.028)		
Height (cm)	0.003	0.005	0.008	0.003	−0.004	0.010*	0.004	0.002
	(0.005)	(0.004)	(0.005)	(0.005)	(0.005)	(0.005)	(0.007)	(0.004)
Years in formal education	−0.031	−0.068***	−0.051*	−0.030	−0.049**	−0.064**	−0.089**	−0.043*
	(0.025)	(0.023)	(0.030)	(0.023)	(0.025)	(0.031)	(0.037)	(0.022)
(educ^2)/100	0.004**	0.004***	0.004**	0.003**	0.007***	0.008***	0.009***	0.007***
	(0.002)	(0.002)	(0.002)	(0.002)	(0.002)	(0.002)	(0.003)	(0.002)
Math score	0.004**	0.003***	0.006***	0.002	0.004*	0.001	0.004*	0.002
	(0.002)	(0.001)	(0.001)	(0.001)	(0.002)	(0.002)	(0.002)	(0.002)
Apprentice (currently)	−0.540***	−0.844***	−0.675***	−0.759***				
	(0.132)	(0.108)	(0.094)	(0.252)				
Apprenticeship completed	−0.044	0.025	0.054	−0.075	0.072	−0.078	0.134	0.025
	(0.072)	(0.065)	(0.072)	(0.064)	(0.128)	(0.121)	(0.109)	(0.101)
Ln (hours)	0.209***	0.170**	0.147*	0.249***	0.137	−0.030	0.318**	−0.008
	(0.081)	(0.083)	(0.076)	(0.080)	(0.116)	(0.117)	(0.161)	(0.091)
Tenure	0.015***	0.010**	0.024***	0.012***	0.009*	0.003	−0.008	0.005
	(0.004)	(0.004)	(0.008)	(0.003)	(0.005)	(0.006)	(0.013)	(0.004)
Ln (employees)	0.301***	0.218***	0.187**	0.313***	0.435***	0.490***	0.001	0.579***
	(0.089)	(0.076)	(0.093)	(0.073)	(0.130)	(0.095)	(0.166)	(0.084)
Ln (firm size)	0.188***	0.163***	0.211***	0.123***	0.223***	0.059*	0.119***	0.136***
	(0.032)	(0.024)	(0.028)	(0.023)	(0.030)	(0.032)	(0.034)	(0.027)
Private wage	−0.267***	−0.319***	−0.372***	−0.119	−0.248**	0.140	−0.179	−0.010
	(0.094)	(0.089)	(0.091)	(0.089)	(0.108)	(0.126)	(0.132)	(0.104)
Civil servant	0.534***	0.473***	0.419***	0.568***	0.377***	0.503***	0.109	0.532***
	(0.136)	(0.113)	(0.138)	(0.104)	(0.116)	(0.128)	(0.144)	(0.094)
Public enterprise	−0.266	−0.219	−0.409**	−0.029	−0.001	0.446**	−0.229	0.329**
	(0.212)	(0.153)	(0.182)	(0.158)	(0.162)	(0.191)	(0.198)	(0.149)
City and year dummies	Yes	Yes	Yes	Yes	Yes	Yes	Yes	Yes
Constant	−0.780	−0.888	−0.992	0.579	9.795***	7.842***	7.202***	9.846***
	(0.894)	(0.783)	(0.855)	(0.855)	(0.992)	(0.963)	(1.358)	(0.742)
R^2	0.256	0.340	0.361	0.236	0.316	0.245	0.252	0.320
Adjusted R^2	0.244	0.328	0.348	0.225	0.295	0.221	0.204	0.306
Number of observations	1,428	1,299	1,073	1,654	716	678	347	1,047

Source: World Bank; values arrived at using the Tanzanian and Ghanaian UPSs.

Note: Standard errors are in parenthesis.

***$p<0.01$ **$p<0.05$ *$p<0.1$

- *Women's earnings also grow slower with age, but peak later in life than those of men.* This finding might reflect lower participation rates among women at a young age and delays in the accumulation of labor market experience.
- *But women experience higher returns to education than men.* Women experience positive returns to having finished primary school, while men only benefit from having finished secondary school and beyond. The result is less pronounced in Tanzania, but is important, because it shows that female schooling can yield higher returns at a young age.
- *Young workers earn significantly less than older workers* in private employment, perhaps because they lack experience and financial capital.
- *Young workers also face the highest unemployment rates.*
- *But returns to education are higher and more highly convex among the young,* suggesting that schooling is more important at the early stages of one's career than later on, when capital accumulation (for example, savings) may help compensate for lack of skills. Skills erosion is another potential explanation for this result.

Differences across Sectors

The specifications presented so far assume that the determinants of earnings are the same across sectors. To investigate whether skills are rewarded differently in different sectors, and to examine how skills vary across sectors, separate earnings functions are presented in table 4.4 for the self-employed, wage employed, and those in public sector employment.

Table 4.4 Earnings Functions by Occupation

	Ghana			Tanzania		
	Self	Private wage	Public wage	Self	Private wage	Public wage
Male	0.317***	0.167***	0.051	0.352***	0.258**	0.165
	(0.079)	(0.062)	(0.129)	(0.071)	(0.102)	(0.107)
Age	0.090***	0.085***	0.019	0.048**	0.005	0.075**
	(0.021)	(0.020)	(0.028)	(0.020)	(0.032)	(0.035)
(age^2)/100	−0.106***	−0.103***	−0.010	−0.053**	0.008	−0.067*
	(0.027)	(0.029)	(0.036)	(0.025)	(0.042)	(0.040)
Height (cm)	0.005	0.005	−0.008	0.003	0.002	0.004
	(0.005)	(0.005)	(0.008)	(0.004)	(0.007)	(0.007)
Years in formal education	0.012	−0.085***	0.000	−0.040	−0.079**	−0.042
	(0.025)	(0.029)	(0.065)	(0.025)	(0.037)	(0.039)
(educ^2)/100	−0.001	0.007***	0.002	0.005**	0.009***	0.006**
	(0.002)	(0.002)	(0.003)	(0.002)	(0.003)	(0.003)
Apprenticeship completed	0.036	−0.057	−0.173	−0.076	0.246	−0.050
	(0.067)	(0.061)	(0.130)	(0.123)	(0.171)	(0.191)

table continues next page

Table 4.4 Earnings Functions by Occupation *(continued)*

	Ghana			Tanzania		
	Self	*Private wage*	*Public wage*	*Self*	*Private wage*	*Public wage*
Apprentice (currently)	−0.415**	−0.802***	−0.313			
	(0.185)	(0.093)	(0.332)			
Math score	0.002	0.004***	0.005**	0.003	−0.000	0.001
	(0.002)	(0.001)	(0.002)	(0.002)	(0.002)	(0.002)
Ln (hours)	0.255***	0.054	0.501**	0.198**	−0.412**	0.171
	(0.074)	(0.092)	(0.212)	(0.098)	(0.164)	(0.248)
Ln (firm size)		0.143***	0.271***		0.154***	0.083
		(0.020)	(0.102)		(0.027)	(0.065)
Tenure	0.012***	0.012**	0.015*	0.004	0.007	−0.003
	(0.004)	(0.005)	(0.009)	(0.006)	(0.006)	(0.006)
Ln (employees)	0.279***			0.465***		
	(0.061)			(0.077)		
Self-employed and not a trader	−0.071			−0.174***		
	(0.066)			(0.067)		
Wage employee in manufacturing		0.014			−0.308***	
		(0.055)			(0.118)	
Public enterprise			−1.263***			−0.109
			(0.475)			(0.176)
City and year dummies	Yes	Yes	Yes	Yes	Yes	Yes
Constant	−1.672**	−0.775	1.392	8.140***	11.457***	7.891***
	(0.832)	(0.871)	(1.610)	(0.826)	(1.455)	(1.699)
Number of observations	1,571	904	225	879	332	175
R^2	0.197	0.534	0.407	0.206	0.374	0.323
Adjusted R^2	0.187	0.523	0.349	0.188	0.335	0.239

Source: World Bank; values arrived at using the Tanzanian and Ghanaian UPSs.
Note: Standard errors are in parenthesis.
***$p<0.01$ **$p<0.05$ *$p<0.1$

The findings show that earnings regimes vary across sectors in a number of ways. For example, the gender gap is highest for the self-employed and statistically negligible for public sector employees. The returns to education also rise more rapidly in wage employment than in self-employment, suggesting higher returns to secondary education for wage workers. However, some interesting commonalities also emerge. For example, the age-earnings profiles of the wage earners and self-employed in Ghana are very similar, unlike those in Tanzania.

Notes

1. As explained in chapter 3, the Raven's test is a cleaner proxy for innate ability than other scores because it measures noncognitive skills, which are arguably less linked to schooling than those measured by the other tests.

2. A young worker is defined as someone younger than the median sample age of 30.

Working toward Better Pay • http://dx.doi.org/10.1596/978-1-4648-0207-2

CHAPTER 5

The Determinants of Earnings Growth

In this chapter we explore the determinant of earnings growth in the Tanzanian and Ghanaian Urban Panel Surveys. We use the panel nature of the data to understand how earnings change over time and how these changes vary across sectors and differ between workers who change sector and those who don't. Box 5.1 sets out our key hypotheses and main findings.

Box 5.1 Key Hypotheses and Main Findings

Hypothesis 1: The variables that determine earnings levels are also strong predictors of changes in earnings.
Main finding: It is difficult to identify predictors of earnings growth.
- The models work poorly in Tanzania and for the Ghanaian self-employed.
- The models work better for wage workers in Ghana.

Hypothesis 2: The determinants of earnings growth vary by sector.
Main finding: The factors governing earnings growth vary substantially across sectors.
- In Ghana, education is positively associated with earnings growth for wage workers, but not for the self-employed.
- Earnings growth is much faster for apprentices than individuals with comparable characteristics.

Hypothesis 3: Switching sectors can lead to substantial changes in earnings.
Main finding: Switching jobs is the main source of earnings growth.
- Moving from small to large firms leads to higher earnings.
- Switching sectors also leads to substantial changes in earnings.
- Moving to the public sector results in gains.
- Moving to self-employment also tends to increase earnings.

Framework

Earnings growth is modeled as a function of changes in the time-variant explanatory variables of earnings levels—that is, firm size, tenure, hours worked, and occupation. Time-invariant characteristics—such as education, gender, and height[1]—are only included as explanatory variables if they are expected to have an additional impact on the rate of earnings *growth* over and above their impact on *levels*. In addition, lagged *levels* of some time-variant variables—for example, firm size—are included to test whether individuals in larger firms/enterprises experience more rapid earnings growth even if their firm does not grow in size. This may be due to large firms raising productivity faster or age-tenure profiles being steeper, as larger firms benefit more from firm-specific skills.[2]

The preferred specification, presented in table 5.1, includes controls for gender, age, height, educational attainment, math test score, and the lag of firm size; a set of variables reflecting changes in hours worked, tenure, firm size; and a set of dummies capturing sector transitions (or the absence thereof), year and city dummies, and dummies indicating whether an individual is entering, graduating, or currently doing an apprenticeship.

Table 5.1 Determinants of One-Year Growth in Log Earnings

Dependent variable: change log earnings	Ghana	Tanzania
Male	−0.005	−0.035
	(0.046)	(0.069)
L.age	0.001	−0.003
	(0.002)	(0.004)
Height (cm)	−0.003	0.001
	(0.003)	(0.005)
Years in formal education	−0.014	−0.001
	(0.017)	(0.024)
(educ^2)/100	0.001	−0.001
	(0.001)	(0.002)
Math score	−0.001	−0.003
	(0.001)	(0.002)
Became apprentice	−0.186	
	(0.260)	
Apprentice, graduated	0.338	
	(0.273)	
L. apprenticeship completed	0.057	−0.002
	(0.043)	(0.099)
L. apprentice (currently)	0.391***	
	(0.127)	
ΔLn (hours)	0.029	0.134
	(0.065)	(0.102)
Δtenure	0.002	0.018*
	(0.005)	(0.010)

table continues next page

Table 5.1 Determinants of One-Year Growth in Log Earnings *(continued)*

Dependent variable: change log earnings	Ghana	Tanzania
L. tenure	0.002	0.003
	(0.003)	(0.005)
ΔLn (employees)	0.095	0.289*
	(0.085)	(0.174)
L.Ln (employees)	−0.003	0.061
	(0.065)	(0.149)
ΔLn (firm size)	0.068***	0.042
	(0.024)	(0.033)
L.Ln (firm size)	0.017	0.015
	(0.016)	(0.029)
Self -> priv wage	0.036	0.091
	(0.154)	(0.228)
Self -> pub wage	0.915	0.649**
	(0.719)	(0.253)
L.priv wage	−0.115*	−0.161
	(0.061)	(0.108)
Priv wage -> self	0.447**	−0.049
	(0.185)	(0.254)
Priv wage -> public	−0.032	−0.043
	(0.100)	(0.149)
L.public	−0.073	0.015
	(0.074)	(0.144)
Public -> self	−0.450	0.028
	(0.327)	(0.149)
Public -> priv wage	−0.224**	−0.220
	(0.111)	(0.304)
Constant	0.693	0.220
	(0.426)	(0.752)
City and year dummies	Yes	Yes
Number of observations	1,461	602
R^2	0.070	0.107
Adjusted R^2	0.050	0.063

Source: World Bank; values arrived at using the Tanzanian and Ghanaian UPSs.
Note: Standard errors are in parenthesis. L. indicates a lagged variable whilst Δ indicates a change in a variable between current and previous time period.
***$p<0.01$ **$p<0.05$ *$p<0.1$

A Bird's Eye View of Earnings Growth in Ghana and Tanzania

Arguably, the most important finding of this analysis is that in both countries it is difficult to predict earnings growth. This is evidenced by the low R^2s of the regressions and the lack of significance of most explanatory variables. These poor results may be due to the very short time horizon over which earnings growth was studied.

Though the R^2s in Tanzania are higher than those in Ghana, the lagged sector of employment and the city dummies (not reported to conserve space) are the only statistically significantly time-invariant variables. Sector changes are also the only significant regressors among those intended to capture the impact of changes in observable characteristics. Although the number of individuals who either became paid apprentices or graduated from a paid apprenticeship was relatively small, some interesting results emerge. Apprentices experience accelerated earnings growth, and graduating from an apprenticeship leads to strongly significant increases in earnings. However, this impact seems to be a one-off event; earnings do not continue to grow faster for workers with apprenticeships, and having finished an apprentice does not lead to higher earnings. Rather, graduation enables the low-paid apprentice to catch up with individuals with comparable observable characteristics.

Switching jobs provides the best opportunity for fast earnings growth. Changes in firm size and sector are also very strongly correlated with increases in earnings, and average earnings growth rates vary across sectors, though the firm size and sectoral effects need to be assessed jointly. In Ghana, losing a public sector job leads to earnings losses, but moving from a private sector wage job to self-employment, on average, increases earnings. In both countries, a move from self-employment to a wage job in a small firm has little impact on earnings, but wages increase when moving to a large firm.

However, it is important to recognize that the ability to find significant predictors of earnings growth may be undermined by the fact that the data are likely to be measured with a substantial degree of noise. Moreover, the fact that earnings change the most as a result of job changes is perhaps not surprising in view of this short time horizon. To examine how sensitive these results are to the time horizon under study, appendix C contains the examination of the determinants of earnings changes over a two-year period. In addition, the analysis attempts to control for possible individual-specific patterns of earnings growth by controlling for fixed effects. Overall, the results do not change very much, though the implied sectoral premia *are* sensitive to the time horizon used.

Differences across Sectors

Thus far, this analysis has imposed a common earnings growth regime across sectors despite the findings of chapter 4, which show that the determinants of earnings *levels* vary across sectors. To examine whether the determinants of earnings *growth* also vary across sectors, we estimate the preferred specification separately for those who started as self-employed, those who started off as wage workers, and those who started in the public sector. Except for wage workers, indicators capturing the impact of becoming an apprentice and graduating from an apprenticeship were dropped since we do not have a sufficient number of observations to identify the effects. Similarly, the sample sizes for public sector employees are small in Ghana and Tanzania, and should thus be interpreted with caution—for completeness they are reported in appendix C, but not discussed in detail. The results of separate earnings regressions for different sectors are presented in table 5.2. Perhaps the most

Table 5.2 Determinants of One-Year Growth in Log Earnings by Occupation

	Ghana			Tanzania		
	Self	Private wage	Public wage	Self	Private wage	Public wage
Male	−0.024	−0.033	0.065	−0.026	0.033	−0.102
	(0.068)	(0.071)	(0.092)	(0.095)	(0.118)	(0.310)
L.age	0.000	0.003	−0.002	−0.000	−0.005	−0.008
	(0.004)	(0.003)	(0.005)	(0.006)	(0.006)	(0.010)
Height (cm)	−0.003	−0.001	−0.007	−0.002	−0.003	0.035*
	(0.003)	(0.004)	(0.007)	(0.007)	(0.006)	(0.020)
Years in formal education	−0.004	−0.056**	−0.100	−0.010	0.023	−0.044
	(0.024)	(0.025)	(0.196)	(0.038)	(0.046)	(0.097)
(educ^2)/100	0.001	0.003**	0.004	0.001	−0.002	−0.001
	(0.002)	(0.001)	(0.008)	(0.004)	(0.004)	(0.007)
Math score	−0.002	−0.002	0.007***	−0.001	−0.005**	0.008
	(0.002)	(0.001)	(0.002)	(0.003)	(0.003)	(0.007)
L.Apprenticeship completed	0.044	0.053	0.029	0.032	−0.234	0.001
	(0.062)	(0.060)	(0.152)	(0.113)	(0.168)	(0.602)
ΔLn (hours)	−0.016	0.274***	0.206	0.112	0.339	0.631
	(0.074)	(0.080)	(0.217)	(0.115)	(0.286)	(0.643)
Δtenure	−0.002	0.022***	−0.008	0.027*	0.020**	0.014
	(0.007)	(0.008)	(0.010)	(0.015)	(0.009)	(0.024)
L.tenure	0.002	0.002	0.009	0.005	0.002	0.007
	(0.004)	(0.005)	(0.006)	(0.007)	(0.006)	(0.016)
ΔLn (employees)	0.059	0.479**		0.281	0.082	
	(0.090)	(0.196)		(0.178)	(0.855)	
L.Ln (employees)	−0.006			0.029		
	(0.070)			(0.150)		
ΔLn (firm size)	0.157	0.099***	−0.001	0.080	0.065	−0.247
	(0.099)	(0.030)	(0.027)	(0.087)	(0.042)	(0.180)
L.Ln (firm size)		0.007	0.019		0.031	−0.042
		(0.020)	(0.023)		(0.030)	(0.159)
Self -> priv wage	−0.181			0.015		
	(0.250)			(0.296)		
Self -> public	0.748			0.627**		
	(0.694)			(0.308)		
becameapp		0.028				
		(0.270)				
Appgrad		0.572**				
		(0.269)				
L.Apprentice (currently)		0.357***				
		(0.125)				
Priv wage -> self		0.340*			−0.148	
		(0.195)			(0.285)	
Priv wage -> public		0.064			0.029	

table continues next page

Table 5.2 Determinants of One-Year Growth in Log Earnings by Occupation *(continued)*

	Ghana			Tanzania		
	Self	*Private wage*	*Public wage*	*Self*	*Private wage*	*Public wage*
		(0.119)			(0.169)	
Public -> self			−0.342			0.706
			(0.233)			(0.592)
Public -> priv wage			−0.126			0.272
			(0.112)			(0.499)
City and year dummies	Yes	Yes	Yes	Yes	Yes	Yes
Constant	0.715	0.494	1.182	0.454	0.974	−5.634*
	(0.583)	(0.709)	(1.610)	(1.050)	(0.957)	(3.371)
Number of observations	897	442	122	404	140	58
R^2	0.057	0.230	0.243	0.134	0.181	0.423

Source: World Bank; values arrived at using the Tanzanian and Ghanaian UPSs.
Note: Standard errors are in parenthesis. L. indicates a lagged variable whilst Δ indicates a change in a variable between current and previous time period.
***$p<0.01$ **$p<0.05$ *$p<0.1$

interesting finding is that these models are much better predictors of earnings growth for wage workers than for the self-employed, at least in Ghana. This is shown by the higher R^2s on the regressions for employees and the fact that more variables are individually significant in Ghana (though not in Tanzania). There are virtually no significant predictors for earnings growth for the self-employed, save for sectoral switches, because it appears that the few individuals who moved from self-employment to a public sector job saw starkly increased earnings. These poor results might be due to higher measurement error in the earnings of the self-employed and the fact that they may include returns to both capital and labor.

The findings for wage workers are more encouraging, at least in Ghana, where education and its square are jointly strongly correlated with educational attainment, suggesting a convex relationship between earnings growth and education. This means that at low levels of education, an additional year of education decelerates earnings growth, but beyond secondary school, earnings grow progressively more with each additional year of education. On the other hand, earnings growth is negatively correlated with cognitive skills, a finding which is difficult to explain. Doing an apprenticeship is again associated with much higher earnings growth during the apprenticeship, and a significant spike in earnings after graduation, but having completed an apprenticeship does not lead to sustained higher earnings growth. Increasing hours worked and moving to a larger firm are also strongly correlated with earnings growth, and individuals who move from wage employment to self-employment tend to experience an increase in earnings that exceeds the benefits of moving to the public sector.

Notes

1. The measure of education and height used in this exercise was constructed to be time invariant (see chapter 3).
2. Note that changes in earnings associated with firm expansion, contraction, or moving between firms of a different size are already controlled for by including changes in firm size as an explanatory variable.

CHAPTER 6

Low-Pay/High-Pay Transitions

In this chapter we focus on low-paid work[1] using the Ghanaian and Tanzanian Urban Panel Surveys. We explore the extent of low-paid work in the survey data and identify whether it is possible for those in low-paid employment to move towards higher paid work. We also analyze the factors associated with moving into and out of low-paying work and whether doing low-paid work has a scarring effect on future earnings. See box 6.1 for the key hypotheses we test in this chapter and our main findings.

Box 6.1 Key Hypotheses and Main Findings

Hypothesis 1: Workers risk being trapped in low-paying occupations, and some groups of workers are particularly at risk of falling into low-pay traps.
Main finding: Low pay is a persistent condition.
- Women and youth are more likely to fall into and remain trapped in low-paying jobs.
- Young women are doubly disadvantaged.

Hypothesis 2: Being in a low-paid job has a scarring effect on prospects of future earnings.
Main finding: The experience of being in a low-paying job is scarring.
- Falling into low pay undermines individuals' prospects of obtaining high-paying jobs in the future.

Hypothesis 3: The process and factors that push individuals out of a low-paying job are not the same as those that pull them out.
Main finding: There is path dependence in pay trajectories.
- The probability of entering/exiting a job category depends on the initial status.

The impact of different factors on the transition probability also depends on both initial and final status.

Descriptive Statistics

Tables 6.1a and 6.1b show that in both Ghana and Tanzania, individuals who were low paid at t-1 are four times more likely to be low paid at time t than other workers. In addition, the average probability of being low paid in two consecutive periods is higher than 50 percent in both countries. The persistence rate is substantially higher than that reported in developed countries and is particularly high for women and for youth.[2] Finally, is it worth noting that a number of t-1 earners have dropped out of the earnings distribution at time t due to either having exited the labor force or simply because of not having reported earnings. Because these individuals are roughly as likely to be low paid as those who stay in the sample, their exit does not bias the results.[3]

Table 6.1a Raw Persistence in Ghana

			Low pay at $t + 1$		
			No	Yes	Total
All	Low pay at t	No	87.14	12.86	100
		Yes	44.78	55.22	100
		Total	72.61	27.39	100
Women	Low pay at t	No	82.13	17.87	100
		Yes	41.79	58.21	100
		Total	65.04	34.96	100
Youth	Low pay at t	No	83.43	16.57	100
		Yes	38.97	61.03	100
		Total	62.9	37.1	100

Table 6.1b Raw Persistence in Tanzania

			Low pay at $t + 1$		
			No	Yes	Total
All	Low pay at t	No	84.78	15.22	100
		Yes	45.71	54.29	100
		Total	70.26	29.74	100
Women	Low pay at t	No	76.36	23.64	100
		Yes	35.22	64.78	100
		Total	56.17	43.83	100
Youth	Low pay at t	No	83.58	16.42	100
		Yes	41.54	58.46	100
		Total	62.88	37.12	100

Source: World Bank; values arrived at using the Tanzanian and Ghanaian UPSs.

Econometric Framework

The descriptive statistics presented above do not allow quantification of the extent to which low-pay persistence is due to the workers who are low paid at time t-1 having systematically lower endowments than the rest—that is, *individual heterogeneity*—as opposed to the experience of low pay itself increasing the probability of being low paid in future—genuine state *dependence* or scarring. The potential scarring effect of being low paid may arise because being in a low-paying job induces human capital depreciation, but also because, in a market with imperfect information, employers might use previous pay as a signal of ability (Cappellari and Jenkins 2004). Being in a low-paying job may also undermine an individual's aspirations and productivity or reduce reservation wages.[4]

However, the sample of low earners at time t-1 is not a random sample of the population, but instead is likely to contain a larger proportion of individuals with a high propensity to be low paid in any period. From the econometric prospective this gives rise to the *initial conditions* problem (Heckman 1981b). An additional econometric challenge is that there may be nonrandom selection into the subsample of individuals for whom two consecutive earnings levels are observed. This is possible because workers with particular characteristics may be relatively more likely to systematically drop out of the sample after the first period.

Modeling Strategy

To address these econometric problems, low-pay/high-pay transitions are modeled using a first-order Markov model that accounts for the initial conditions problem and nonrandom retention. The modeling framework is an adaptation of the framework used by Cappellari and Jenkins (2004), who treat selection into base-year earnings category and sample retention as issues of multiple endogenous selection. An appealing feature of this approach is that it is a switching model that allows the determinants of low pay to have a differential impact, depending on whether the individual in question was in a low-paying or high-paying job in the previous period. In other words, the model helps examine whether the effects of individual characteristics—such as age, gender, and education—on the probability of moving out of a low-paying job differ from their impacts on the probability of falling into low-paying employment.

However, a very severe limitation of this modeling strategy is that it imposes very strong structural assumptions. More specifically, the approach used multivariate probit models to model low-earnings transitions between two consecutive years, pooling observations across observed transitions. The most general model comprises three equations: (i) an initial conditions equation that models base-year low pay, (ii) a retention equation that determines whether wages are observed both in period t-1 and in period t, and (iii) a transition equation that models low-pay status in period t. These equations are assumed to have a common error process. The correlations between the error terms in the different equations are used to account for unobserved heterogeneity—as explained in more detail in appendix D.

Model Specification and Performance

The bivariate specification of earnings transitions uses personal characteristics (education, gender, age, height, and whether the person has ever been an apprentice) and job characteristics (sector dummies, tenure, firm size, or number of employees) to control for the initial conditions. Year dummies are used to control for transitions due to systematic increases in earnings associated with time trends, such as technical progress. Dummies for current city are also included and parental education is used as an instrument for the initial conditions equation, although it may itself be correlated with the probability of transiting. Tests of alternative specifications are presented in appendix D.

The estimated correlation between unobservables in the two equations is negative in both countries, though insignificant in Tanzania, probably because of the relatively small number of transitions. This suggests that there is "regression to the mean" in the sense that individuals who were low paid at t-1 are more likely to be high paid this year, potentially reflecting error in the measure of earnings.

Results

These models help examine how personal and job characteristics impinge on the probability of moving from low-paying to high-paying jobs and vice versa. The endogenous switching model implies that regressors have different effects, depending on whether the analysis is conditioning on high or low pay. Since we are most interested in low pay, the analysis focused on the low-income persistence rate s_{it} (the probability of being low paid at t, conditional on being low paid at t-1) and the low-income entry rate e_{it} (the probability of being low paid at t, conditional on being high paid at t-1). Appendix D explains how to compute these rates. The analysis also documented expected durations of high-paid and low-paid employment spells under the assumption that the economic environment is stationary, that is, it does not change over time. In addition, the models measured state dependence.

The Determinants of Transition Probabilities

The analysis explored the impact on the predicted probabilities of low-pay persistence and entry (s_{it} and e_{it}), allowing personal and job characteristics to vary. The results for Ghana are shown in table 6.3 and those for Tanzania in table 6.4.

Two broad messages emerge from the findings. The first important message is the existence of significant evidence of path dependence in low-pay/high-pay transitions in both countries. This is shown by the fact that the impact of the explanatory variables on low-pay persistence probabilities is not statistically equal to that on the propensity to remain in (relatively) high-pay employment. The second important findings is that there is also cross-country and within-country heterogeneity in persistence and entry rates of low pay and in their determinants.

In Ghana, if high-paid at t–1, the reference individual has a predicted probability of 13 percent of entering low-paid employment in the next period (first

Table 6.2a Predicted Entry and Persistence Rates, and Mean and Median Predicted Time in High and Low Pay for Ghana, Bivariate

	Low entry (%)	Mean high	Median high	Low persist (%)	Mean low	Median low
Reference	13	7.6	4.9	50	2.0	1.0
Educ = 12	10	9.9	6.5	51	2.0	1.0
Female	23	4.3	2.6	59	2.4	1.3
Small firm	12	8.6	5.6	47	1.9	0.9
Public employee	7	14.9	10.0	44	1.8	0.8
Age = 40	11	9.3	6.1	43	1.8	0.8
Apprentice	12	8.2	5.3	50	2.0	1.0
Tenure	14	7.3	4.7	46	1.8	0.9
1 employee	9	11.0	7.3	49	2.0	1.0
Age = 20	21	4.8	3.0	63	2.7	1.5

Table 6.2b Predicted Entry and Persistence Rates, and Mean and Median Predicted Time in High and Low Pay for Tanzania, Bivariate

	Low entry (%)	Mean high	Median high	Low persist (%)	Mean low	Median low
Reference individual	10	10.2	6.7	24	1.3	0.5
Educ = 12	1	78.4	54.0	2	1.0	0.2
Female	22	4.6	2.8	61	2.5	1.4
Small firm	7	14.3	9.6	46	1.8	0.9
Public employee	3	38.8	26.5	6	1.1	0.3
Age = 40	11	9.3	6.1	16	1.2	0.4
Apprentice	10	10.2	6.7	15	1.2	0.4
Tenure	8	11.8	7.8	26	1.4	0.5
1 employee	6	17.4	11.7	24	1.3	0.5
Age = 20	10	10.0	6.6	40	1.7	0.8

Source: World Bank; values arrived at using the Tanzanian and Ghanaian UPSs.
Notes: The reference person is a 30-year-old, self-employed male with no employees, who has seven years of education, five years of tenure in his current job, and never been an apprentice. Low entry refers to the probability of being low paid in the next period conditional on being high paid currently. Low persist refers to the probability of continuing to be low paid in the next period.

column of table 6.2a). By contrast, the fourth column shows that, if low paid at time t–1, the reference individual has a 50 percent probability of remaining in low-paid employment. As shown in Table 6.2b, the gap is somewhat smaller in Tanzania, but still significant (10 and 24 percent, respectively).

Tables 6.2a and 6.2b also show how the probability varies with personal and job characteristics. The low-pay entry rate is higher in Ghana than in Tanzania, but the difference is particularly striking for the persistence rate, which is more than double. Ghana also shows higher within-group heterogeneity in the low-income entry rates, whereas in Tanzania, heterogeneity in persistence rates is higher. In so far as policies concentrate on the low earners, these might have higher payoffs in Tanzania. For Ghana, these results suggest substantial potential payoffs to targeting the earners most at risk of transitioning into the low-paid employment categories, particularly youth and women. This conclusion is strengthened by the work below on measuring state dependence.

In line with the findings in the previous sections of this study regarding large returns to education, in Tanzania the largest estimated source of heterogeneity is education. Having 12 years of schooling lowers the probability of entering low pay and of low-pay persistence by more than 90 percent, and this dramatically increases the mean predicted years out of low-pay. By contrast, the strongest effects in Ghana are observed for youth and women, who are nearly twice as likely to fall into low-pay employment and, respectively, 20 and 26 percent more likely to get trapped in it. Young women are doubly disadvantaged. Women face heavy disadvantage in Tanzania too. They are more than twice as likely as men to fall into low pay and 40 percent more likely to remain trapped. Interestingly, the large disadvantage seen for youth in Tanzania is only evident for those already in low pay (60 percent above that of the reference category), while the probability of entry into it (for those who are better paid) is not significantly different. Results from both countries also confirm the advantage of being employed in the public sector: the probability of a public sector employee entering low pay is half that of the reference individual, and the expected persistence in this status is also much lower. The probabilities of entry into low pay are also substantially lower for the self-employed with employees.

Testing for Evidence of Labor Market Scarring

The descriptive statistics presented above also give us a very crude measure of state dependence that does not control for differences between individuals, either observed or unobserved. To control for these factors, we compute two alternative measures of state dependence: aggregate state dependence (ASD) and genuine state dependence (GSD).[5]

Using the bivariate specification, the ASD is estimated to be 0.42 in Ghana and 0.45 in Tanzania, while GSD values for both countries are 0.35 and 0.27, respectively. When using the trivariate model to control for retention, both ASD and GSD values are significantly reduced in Ghana, to 0.27 and 0.23, respectively. Overall, these results suggest that there *are* substantial scarring effects of low pay in both Tanzania and Ghana. The values for GSD are similar to those reported for developed countries, but the ASD figures are generally lower. For example, Cappellari (2002), using panel data on Italian workers, finds a GSD value between 0.20 and 0.36, but ASD values between 0.49 and 0.61, depending on specification. The lower ASD values suggest higher mobility across the low-income line in the African economies than in developed countries, in accordance with the existence of a larger group of individuals vulnerable to low earnings.[6] However, measurement error may also be a more severe problem in developing country data sets than in developed country data. The fact that ASD is closer to GSD in Ghana and Tanzania than in other countries suggests that scarring plays a larger role than observable characteristics.

Notes

1. *Low-paid jobs* are those that pay less than US$1.25 a day. For more details, see chapter 3. The alternative definition of 60 percent of median earnings was used to assess the robustness of the results, but since the conclusions were not qualitatively different, these results are not reported to conserve space.

2. The higher persistence rate compared to developed countries may partly reflect the different low-pay line used (Stewart and Swaffield 1999).

3. Results are available from the authors.

4. The *reservation wage* is the lowest wage rate at which a worker would be willing to accept a particular type of job. A job offer involving the same type of work and the same working conditions, but at a lower wage rate, would be rejected by the worker.

5. Following Cappellari and Jenkins (2004), ASD is defined as the difference between the probability of being low paid at t, for those low paid at $t-1$, and the probability of being low paid at t, for those *not* low paid at $t-1$. GSD is defined as the average difference between the predicted probabilities of being low paid conditional on being low paid and high paid, respectively. Measures of ASD are arguably less prone to measurement error than measures of raw state dependence. However, contrary to the GSD, they do not control for individual heterogeneity. If differences in observed individual characteristics are the main drivers of initial pay states and transitions between states, the GSD is expected to be lower than ASD, and, in the presence of labor market scarring, the GSD should be greater than zero.

6. Though it should be remembered very different low-income lines are used in the literature on developed countries.

CHAPTER 7

Main Findings and Key Policy Implications

This study contributes to understanding earnings dynamics in low-income countries (LICs) by examining the determinants of earnings, earnings growth, and low-pay/high-pay transitions in Ghana and Tanzania. It highlights the importance of personal and job characteristics in determining earnings and earnings growth, but also finds large variations across sectors and firm size in the returns to individual characteristics and the prospects for earnings growth. These findings point toward strong path dependence in pay trajectories and the existence of a scarring effect. Thus, falling into low-pay employment reduces considerably one's future labor market prospects. These results go beyond the time period covered by the data (2004–08) and also have a number of important implications for the potential effectiveness of alternative interventions in enhancing the quality of employment opportunities, not only in Ghana and Tanzania, but also in LICs more broadly.

Message 1: Job Characteristics Are an Important Determinant of Both Earnings Levels and Earnings Growth

In the short run, the most effective way of increasing earnings is to change the type of job, because earnings and potential for growth vary considerably across different types of employment. Returns to education, in terms of both earnings levels and growth, also seem driven to a large extent by differences in the type of jobs available to workers of different ages and education. The scope for wage increases within a given job is much more limited. In addition, the persistence in earnings is high and the initial employment type is an important determinant of where one ends up. Being in a low-paying job has powerful scarring effects that make it difficult to move to better-paid job. Thus, individual earnings trajectories are to a large extent determined by one's labor allocation across sectors over the life cycle.

Policy implication: Introducing measures that act as safety ropes and prevent vulnerable individuals from falling into low-pay might yield high returns, since it is more difficult to get people out of low-paying jobs once they have fallen into them.

Message 2: Women and Youth Face Special Challenges

Women and young workers earn much less than men and older workers, even after controlling for educational disadvantages. They are also much less likely to escape low-paying jobs and have higher risk of falling into low pay.

Policy implication: Gender-sensitive and youth-focused social protection policies are a first step to bridging the gender and youth gaps in earnings.

Message 3: Skills Acquisition Is a Stepping Stone Toward Better Paying Jobs, at Least in Wage Employment, Especially for Women

As in previous studies, this analysis finds a strong correlation between skills acquisition - proxied by education, cognitive skills, and having completed an apprenticeship - and initial earnings. However, the relationship between skills and earnings growth is much weaker, although it varies across employment type. In Ghana, education is significantly positively correlated with earnings growth for the wage employed, but not for the self-employed. In both countries, the returns to education are higher for women.

Policy implication: Existing efforts to raise educational attainment may yield high returns and promoting female school enrollment may be especially beneficial. In addition, the finding that returns to education are increasing and robust, even when controlling for ability bias, suggests that investing in tertiary education might be an excellent means of capitalizing on the gains of enhanced primary and secondary school completion rates.[1]

Message 4: Self-Employment Can Be Desirable

Although different sectors offer different returns, being self-employed is not always synonymous with having low earnings. Indeed, on average, moves into wage employment are just as likely to lead to better pay as moves to self-employment. This supports the view that self-employment is not always employment of the last resort. Yet, entrepreneurs are on average older than wage workers, hinting at the possibility of capital constraints.

Policy implication: Facilitating better access to credit might be beneficial.

Message 5: The Public Sector Wage Premium Is a Potential Barrier to the Efficient Working of the Labor Market

Civil servants earn more than private sector employees with comparable characteristics, and, unsurprisingly, moves into the public sector are associated with increased earnings, while moves out of it tend to be associated with a wage drop. This suggests that public sector jobs may be rationed. This hypothesis is consistent with the finding that a large percentage of those not working at the time of the surveys are highly educated individuals likely to be queuing for public sector jobs.

Policy implication: Reducing the public sector pay premium by stalling earnings increases can contribute to a less distorted labor market.

Note

1. Of course, these arguments implicitly assume that the returns to education remain constant-which may not be the case if tertiary school enrollment rates increased rapidly or if girls' educational attainment caught up with that of boys.

Summary Statistics and Variable Definitions

Summary Statistics

Table A.1 Summary Statistics (Ghana)

Variable	Mean	Observations
Male	0.43	6,796
Age	31.32	6,455
Education	8.75	6,795
Height	164.00	6,422
Math score	45.88	5,482
Raven's score	32.96	4,218
English score	60.28	5,511
Reading score	55.88	4,605
Apprenticeship completed	0.28	6,813
Apprentice (currently)	0.05	6,509
Employees	1.25	3,864
Firm size	13.13	3,819
Hours	46.74	3,994
Tenure	8.43	3,884

Source: World Bank; values arrived at using the Tanzanian and Ghanaian UPSs.

Table A.2 Summary Statistics (Tanzania)

Variable	Mean	Observations
Male	0.46	2,412
Age	35.81	2,413
Education	5.05	2,413
Height	163.97	2,197
Math score	61.11	2,233
Raven's score	19.09	1,848
English score	64.79	1,751
Reading score	59.99	2,163

table continues next page

Table A.2 Summary Statistics (Tanzania) *(continued)*

Variable	Mean	Observations
Apprenticeship completed	0.07	2,413
Employees	0.14	1,090
Firm size	20.20	1,702
Hours	52.47	1,711
Tenure	9.80	1,899

Source: World Bank; values arrived at using the Tanzanian and Ghanaian UPSs.

Table A.3 Mean (1-Year) Changes in Log Earnings by Transition Type (Ghana)

Transition	Mean change	Number of trans
SE w/o -> SE w/o	0.194	750
SE w/o -> SE w	0.486	98
SE w/o -> W <=10	0.387	62
SE w/o -> W >10	0.791	16
SE w/o -> Civil	0.263	2
SE w/o -> Pub Ent	2.661	1
SE w -> SE w/o	0.244	59
SE w -> SE w	−0.010	143
SE w -> W <=10	−0.703	4
SE w -> W >10	0.328	7
SE w -> Civil	2.235	1
W <=10 -> SE w/o	0.617	34
W <=10 -> SE w	1.027	13
W <=10 -> W <=10	0.149	162
W <=10 -> W >10	0.263	52
W <=10 -> Civil	−0.022	3
W <=10 -> Pub Ent	−0.631	1
W >10 -> SE w/o	−0.104	11
W >10 -> SE w	1.845	3
W >10 -> W <=10	0.082	21
W >10 -> W >10	0.083	215
W >10 -> Civil	0.035	7
W >10 -> Pub Ent	0.307	6
Civil -> SE w/o	−0.502	3
Civil -> W <=10	0.384	1
Civil -> W >10	0.105	7
Civil -> Civil	0.030	66
Civil -> Pub Ent	0.025	4
Pub Ent -> SE w/o	−0.234	2
Pub Ent -> SE w	0.345	1
Pub Ent -> W <=10	−0.117	3
Pub Ent -> W >10	0.000	12

table continues next page

Table A.3 Mean (1-Year) Changes in Log Earnings by Transition Type (Ghana) *(continued)*

Transition	Mean change	Number of trans
Pub Ent -> Civil	0.171	14
Pub Ent -> Pub Ent	0.136	26
Total	0.195	1,810

Source: World Bank; values arrived at using the Tanzanian and Ghanaian UPSs.
Note: SE w/o = self-employed without employees; SE w = self-employed with employees; W <=10 = wage employee working in a firm with 10 employees or less; W>10 = wage employee working in a firm with more than 10 employees; Civil = Civil servant; Pub Ent = public enterprise.

Table A.4 Mean (1-Year) Changes in Log Earnings by Transition Type (Tanzania)

Transition	Mean change	Number of trans
SE w/o -> SE w/o	0.184	285
SE w/o -> SE w	0.455	44
SE w/o -> W <=10	0.568	7
SE w/o -> W >10	0.392	9
SE w/o -> Civil	0.531	4
SE w/o -> Pub En	1.184	2
SE w -> SE w/o	0.111	28
SE w -> SE w	0.049	26
SE w -> W <=10	−0.289	1
SE w -> W >10	−1.511	1
SE w -> Civil	.	0
W <=10 -> SE w/o	0.418	3
W <=10 -> SE w	0.019	2
W <=10 -> W <=10	0.134	28
W <=10 -> W >10	−0.020	17
W <=10 -> Civil	0.656	7
W <=10 -> Pub Ent	−0.023	2
W >10 -> SE w/o	−0.639	2
W >10 -> W <=10	0.038	10
W >10 -> W >10	0.171	34
W >10 -> Civil	−0.090	23
W >10 -> Pub Ent	0.036	14
Civil -> W <=10	−1.106	2
Civil -> W >10	0.196	6
Civil -> Civil	−0.016	18
Civil -> Pub Ent	1.839	2
Pub Ent -> SE w/o	−0.070	2
Pub Ent -> W <=1	−0.016	4
Pub Ent -> W >10	−0.056	5
Pub Ent -> Civil	0.084	9
Pub Ent -> Pub Ent	0.037	11
Total	0.169	608

Source: World Bank; values arrived at using the Tanzanian and Ghanaian UPSs.
Note: SE w/o = self-employed without employees; SE w = self-employed with employees; W <=10 = wage employee working in a firm with 10 employees or less; W>10 = wage employee working in a firm with more than 10 employees; Civil = Civil servant; Pub Ent = public enterprise.

Variable Definitions

Education

This is a continuous variable derived from assigning a number of years equivalent-based on the structure of the school systems in Ghana and Tanzania-to the highest educational attainment reported.

Firm Size

This variable captures the number of workers, including the respondent, who work in the same firm. For self-employed entrepreneurs, it is set to 0.

Height

The variable is constructed to be time invariant by averaging observations on height over time. This helps to smooth measurement error.

Tenure

This variable is constructed by calculating the number of years between the start of current job-as recalled by the respondent-and the date of the interview.

Number of Employees

Self-employed entrepreneurs are asked to report the total number of people they employ in their business, including both household members (paid or unpaid) and non-household members. The variable is set to 1 for the self-employed entrepreneurs who don't hire any employees and for all wage workers (in the public and private sector).

A Framework for Analyzing Earnings Panel Data

The starting point is the following semilogarithmic model of earnings:

$$y_{it} = \alpha_0 + \alpha_1 X_{1it} + \alpha_2 X_{2i} + u_i + \varepsilon_{it} \tag{B.1}$$

where:

y_{it} is the natural logarithm of net monthly income.
X_{1it} is a vector of time-variant determinants of earnings (including common time trends).
X_{2i} is a vector of time-invariant determinants of earnings.
u_i is a time-invariant, individual-specific determinant of earnings.
ε_{it} is a time-varying error term.

Ordinary least squares (OLS) estimates of equation (B.1) (presented in table 4.2) will be unbiased and consistent if both time-variant and time-invariant determinants of earnings are uncorrelated with the time-invariant (OLS A1) and time-variant (OLS A2) components of the residual:

(OLS A1): $\qquad\qquad E[X_{1it}\varepsilon_{it}] = E[X_{2i}\varepsilon_{it}] = 0$

(OLS A2): $\qquad\qquad E[X_{1it}u_i] = E[X_{2i}u_i] = 0$

Tackling the Endogeneity of Schooling

We ignore the role of the time-invariant fixed effects u_i for the time being, and focus on the potential violations of assumption OLS A1 due to the potential endogeneity of education, which might arise if educational attainment is correlated with unobserved ability and ability affects earnings. In such a scenario, OLS estimates of equation (B.1) will be biased (since $E[X_{1it}\varepsilon_{it}] \neq 0$). To correct for this potential bias, we use two approaches; the preferred approach is to control for ability *directly*, by including measures of cognitive skills, which we use as proxies.

In addition, we use a control function (CF) approach, where the residual of a model of educational attainment is used as a regressor in the earnings equation.

The idea behind the CF approach is to model the dependence between the unobserved error terms in such a way that the endogeneity bias disappears. The model of educational attainment, E_i, is presented in table B.1 and uses distance to primary school at age 6 and distance to secondary school at age 16 as exclusion restrictions, Z_i, that is, they are assumed to be correlated with education and do not have a direct impact on earnings (that is, once education is controlled for, they do not have any additional impact on earnings). In addition, the model controls for the individual's age and gender. The estimable equation thus becomes:

$$E_{it} = \varphi_0 + \varphi_1 X_{1it} + \varphi_2 X_{2i} + \varphi_3 Z_i + \eta_{it} \qquad (B.2)$$

Predicted residuals from the first-stage regression are then used as controls for unobserved factors affecting both earnings and education in an earnings specification that is equal to equation (B.1) in all other respects.

$$y_{it} = \alpha_0 + \alpha_1 X_{1it} + \alpha_2 X_{2i} + \hat{\eta}_{it} + u_i + \varepsilon_{it} \qquad (B.3)$$

where:

$$\hat{\eta}_{it} = E_{it} - (\hat{\varphi}_0 + \hat{\varphi}_1 X_{1it} + \hat{\varphi}_2 X_{2i} + \hat{\varphi}_3 Z_i)$$

As shown by Wooldridge (2007), under the rather stringent assumptions that:

$$E\left(\varepsilon_{it} | X_{1it}, X_{2i}, Z_i, E_{it}\right) = E\left(\varepsilon_{it} | X_{1it}, X_{2i}, Z_i, \eta_{it}\right) = E\left(\varepsilon_{it} | \eta_{it}\right) = \rho \; \eta_{it}$$

estimates of α_0, α_1, and α_2 will now be unbiased. Note that the first equality holds because E_{it} and η_{it} are one-to-one functions of each other. The second equality holds if $(\varepsilon_{it}, \eta_{it})$ is independent of (X_{1it}, X_{2i}, Z_i) and if we are willing to assume linearity in the conditional expectation $E\left(\varepsilon_{it} | \eta_{it}\right)$. Both these conditions are nontrivial, but generate an estimator that is more efficient than standard IV in nonlinear models.

Controlling for Unobserved Fixed Effects

In section B.2, we relax the second of the identification assumptions and allow for potential correlation between fixed effects u_i and observable determinants of earnings, X_{1it} and X_{2i}:

$$E[X_{1it} u_i] \neq 0; \; E[X_{2i} u_i] \neq 0$$

Instead, we use two alternative assumptions. First, we assume that the time-variant determinant of earnings is uncorrelated with time-variant unobservables *at any other point in time.*

(WG A1): $E[X_{1is} \varepsilon_{it}] = 0 \; \forall \; s, t$

Table B.1 Control Function Approach to Instrument Education and Apprenticeships (First Stage)

Country	Ghana		Tanzania	
	Coef/SE	Coef/SE	Coef/SE	Coef/SE
Estimation method	OLS	Probit	OLS	Probit
Dependent variable:	Educational attainment	Completed an apprenticeship?	Educational attainment	Completed an apprenticeship?
Male	1.604***	0.144	0.245	−0.059
	(0.257)	(0.092)	(0.308)	(0.137)
Age	0.297***	0.014	0.146	0.153***
	(0.076)	(0.028)	(0.093)	(0.049)
(age^2)/100	−0.428***	−0.032	−0.243**	−0.164***
	(0.103)	(0.038)	(0.118)	(0.060)
Distance to the nearest primary school at age 6	0.024**	−0.001	−0.010	−0.005
	(0.012)	(0.004)	(0.012)	(0.006)
Distance to the nearest secondary school at age 16	−0.015***	−0.001	−0.430*	−0.027
	(0.005)	(0.002)	(0.255)	(0.111)
Constant	3.405**	−0.665	4.242**	−4.434***
	(1.343)	(0.487)	(1.825)	(1.008)
Number of observations	866	866	766	766
R^2	0.075		0.028	
Pseudo R^2		0.01		0.05

Source: World Bank; values arrived at using the Tanzanian and Ghanaian UPSs.
Note: Coef = coefficient; SE = standard error; OLS = ordinary least squares.
***p<0.01   **p<0.05   *p<0.1

This assumption will allow us to employ a within-group estimator, which is effectively equivalent to OLS on the following transformed model:

$$\tilde{y}_{it} = \alpha_1 \tilde{X}_{1it} + \tilde{\varepsilon}_{it} \tag{B.4}$$

where $\tilde{y}_{it} = y_{it} - \frac{1}{T}\sum_{1}^{T} y_{it}$, $\tilde{X}_{1it} = X_{1it} - \frac{1}{T}\sum_{1}^{T} X_{1it}$ and $\tilde{\varepsilon}_{it} = \varepsilon_{it} - \frac{1}{T}\sum_{1}^{T} \varepsilon_{it}$. It should

be noted that in small samples $\tilde{\varepsilon}_{it}$ is negatively correlated with $\tilde{X}_{1it}$ by construction, leading to the Nickell bias (Nickell 1981), which is typically in the opposite direction of the bias in the OLS estimator.

Second, we make the less restrictive assumption that the time-variant determinants of earnings are uncorrelated with time-variant unobservables only in the same and in the previous period.

(FD A1): $E[X_{1it}\varepsilon_{it-1}] = E[X_{1it-1}\varepsilon_{it}] = 0$

This second variant will justify the estimation of the following model in first differences, using OLS regressions.

$$\Delta y_{it} = \alpha_1 \Delta X_{1it} + \Delta \varepsilon_{it} \tag{B.5}$$

Since first differences are not available for the first sample wave, this leads to a reduction in sample size, and, consequently, less precise estimates.

Sorting Matters, But Is Not the Entire Story

If time-invariant determinants of earnings that are unobserved yet correlated with the explanatory variables exist, the OLS estimates may be biased. For example, the sector differentials may simply reflect differences in unobserved ability. By first differencing the earnings regressions ("first difference [FD] estimator") or using fixed effects estimation (the "within-group estimator" or "fixed effect [FE] estimator"), one can control for such individual-specific unobservables. However, as explained in section B.1, this comes at a cost, because we are then no longer able to assess the impact of time-invariant variables on earnings. In addition, the fixed effects estimator might be downward biased due to the fact that, by construction, the error terms are correlated with the regressors (the so-called Nickell bias). While the FD estimator does not suffer from the same drawback, it does lead to reductions in sample size and, consequently, less precise estimates. Yet, we still prefer the latter over the FE estimators since it yields unbiased estimates. Since first-differenced estimates examine the determinants of earnings *changes* as a function of *changes* in observable characteristics, they also provide a first-pass at the determinants of earnings growth.

Table B.2 presents the results of earnings functions estimated by means of fixed effects estimation (columns 1 and 4) and using the within group estimator (columns 2 and 5). The regressions only include time-varying observable characteristics. Note that we have dropped age, since, by construction, the change in age from one year to the next will be constant.

Overall, the results do not change very much compared to the OLS specifications. To start with, the estimated firm-size effect is relatively robust to controlling for fixed effects, suggesting that the initial observation that workers in large firms earn more than those in small firms is correct. The fact that the effect is lower than in the OLS specifications suggests it partially reflects sorting of more able individuals into larger firms (see the discussion in the review of the related literature in chapter 2). Turning to sectoral premia, the results from the within-group estimation show a strong and significant civil service premium in Ghana and a strong public enterprise premium in Tanzania. The effect of working in the private sector, although of the same sign as in previous regressions, does not appear significant. In sum, these results suggest that sectoral premia reflect both sorting across sectors and genuine differences in remuneration between sectors.

Table B.2 Earnings Functions (FE and FD)

Country	Ghana			Tanzania		
Estimation method	FE	FD(1)	FD(2)	FE	FD(1)	FD(2)
	Coef/SE	Coef/SE	Coef/SE	Coef/SE	Coef/SE	Coef/SE
(age^2)/100	−0.008	−0.017	0.001	0.040*	0.029**	0.031**
	(0.090)	(0.077)	(0.080)	(0.024)	(0.014)	(0.014)
Ln (hours)	0.176**	0.076	0.079	0.138	0.132	0.147
	(0.074)	(0.065)	(0.065)	(0.155)	(0.103)	(0.101)
Tenure	0.004	0.000	0.001	0.009	0.015*	0.014*
	(0.005)	(0.005)	(0.005)	(0.009)	(0.008)	(0.009)
Ln (employees)	0.161*	0.133*	0.123*	0.244	0.255**	0.247*
	(0.089)	(0.073)	(0.073)	(0.171)	(0.126)	(0.127)
Ln (firm size)	0.125***	0.082***	0.084***	0.065*	0.045**	0.051*
	(0.037)	(0.032)	(0.031)	(0.036)	(0.021)	(0.026)
Priv wage	−0.256**	−0.169		0.123	0.184	
	(0.126)	(0.116)		(0.196)	(0.137)	
Civil service	0.312*	0.241		0.101	0.146	
	(0.177)	(0.153)		(0.257)	(0.206)	
Public enterprise	−0.166	−0.056		0.176	0.254	
	(0.198)	(0.163)		(0.278)	(0.179)	
Self -> priv wage			0.019			0.044
			(0.138)			(0.196)
Self -> civil			0.538			0.337
			(0.821)			(0.259)
Self -> Pub Ent			2.067***			0.903***
			(0.162)			(0.171)
Priv wage -> priv wage			−0.077**			−0.094
			(0.031)			(0.069)
Priv wage -> self			0.533***			−0.131
			(0.166)			(0.221)
Priv wage -> civil			−0.006			−0.088
			(0.138)			(0.141)
Priv wage -> Pub Ent			−0.202			−0.191*
			(0.168)			(0.099)
Civil -> civil			−0.133**			−0.132
			(0.066)			(0.088)
Civil -> self			−0.620***			
			(0.148)			
Civil -> priv wage			−0.497**			−0.230
			(0.208)			(0.627)
Civil -> Pub Ent			−0.621***			1.726
			(0.229)			(1.337)
Pub Ent -> Pub Ent			0.002			−0.122*
			(0.089)			(0.072)

table continues next page

Table B.2 Earnings Functions (FE and FD) *(continued)*

Country		Ghana			Tanzania	
Estimation method	FE	FD(1)	FD(2)	FE	FD(1)	FD(2)
	Coef/SE	Coef/SE	Coef/SE	Coef/SE	Coef/SE	Coef/SE
Pub Ent -> self			−0.016			−0.131
			(0.370)			(0.332)
Pub Ent -> priv wage			−0.205**			−0.174
			(0.103)			(0.131)
Pub Ent -> civil			0.326			0.043
			(0.209)			(0.194)
Year dummies	Yes	Yes	Yes	Yes	Yes	Yes
Constant	1.628	0.184**	0.168**	9.387***	0.119**	0.142***
	(1.140)	(0.074)	(0.076)	(0.719)	(0.049)	(0.055)
Number of observations	3,454	1,753	1,753	1,604	610	610
R^2	0.150	0.043	0.060	0.113	0.043	0.063
Adjusted R^2	0.147	0.037	0.047	0.108	0.028	0.031

Source: World Bank; values arrived at using the Tanzanian and Ghanaian UPSs.

Note: Coef = coefficient; SE = standard error. FD = first difference; FE = fixed effect. NB First differenced estimates use the first difference of the dependent variable as well as first differenced explanatory variables; for example, Ln (employees) is in fact ΔLn (employees). FE and FD estimates are presented alongside each other to conserve space.

***$p<0.01$

**$p<0.05$

*$p<0.1$

What Do These Regressions Tell Us About Growth? Asymmetric Sectoral Switching Premia

The FD estimator can be interpreted as a growth regression because it examines the determinants of earnings *changes*. Both the within-group estimator and the FD specification have implicitly assumed symmetry in the effect of sector switching. In other words, the effects of going in and out of a certain sector have implicitly been assumed to be reciprocal. Because this is a strong restriction, we set out to test it. Column 3 shows the results of an FD estimation (similar to that used for column 2), where we substituted the first differences of sectoral dummies with switch-specific dummies, capturing the effect of moving from one particular sector into another, thus allowing for asymmetric effects of switching between sectors. Tables A.3 and A.4 presented descriptive data on the amount of sector switching and demonstrated that most people gain from doing so. Here we control for their observable characteristics, thus examining whether changes in earnings reflect changes in observable characteristics or pure sector effects.

The results demonstrate that the effects documented above are robust when controlling for changes in time-varying observable characteristics. Moving from the private sector to self-employment has a strong positive effect on earnings, yet moving in the opposite direction does not have an effect of the opposite sign. In fact, once we account for the effect of the increase in firm size that derives from moving from self-employment to private sector employment, this switch has itself a positive effect. Some evidence of symmetry, on the other hand, seems to exist for movements in and out of the public service; movements into the public sector are associated with substantial pay rises, while movements out of it are associated with significant pay cuts. The number of such switches, however, is too low to heavily rely on these results. Parallel results for Tanzania are included for completeness, but due to the smaller sample size, the number of switches observed is too small to make substantive conclusions.

A Framework for Analyzing Earnings Growth

Econometric Framework

The framework starts from the following general growth model:

$$y_{it} = \alpha_0 + \lambda y_{i,t-1} + \alpha_1 X_{1it} + \alpha_2 X_{2i} + \alpha_3 X_{2i} \cdot time + u_i + \rho_i \cdot time + \varepsilon_{it} \quad (C.1)$$

where both time-varying X_{1it} and time-invariant X_{2i} observables have an impact on earnings. The crucial difference with the model in levels presented in chapter 4 is an explicit treatment of income dynamics by including income in the previous period among the explanatory variables. Moreover, by allowing time-invariant observables X_{2i} to have a different impact on earning levels at different points in time (hence the interaction term $\alpha_3 X_{2i} \cdot time$), one can test whether personal and job characteristics impact *earnings growth*.

As pointed out by Deaton (1997, 110), in short panels, it is very difficult to distinguish between persistence in earnings due to unobserved individual heterogeneity (as captured in u_i and ρ_i) and persistence due to the effect of the lagged dependent variables, as captured by λ. Differencing equation (C.1) helps get rid of the fixed effect u_i, yet also induces serial correlation in the error term, which will yield a downward bias in ordinary least squares (OLS) estimates of λ. This observation is a key concern in the large literature on earnings convergence, which typically finds strong evidence for high persistence and regression to the mean. To circumvent the identification problems that introduction of the lagged dependent variable would entail, we make the very strong assumption that changes in earnings are fully persistent, that is, that $\lambda = 1$. This assumption is restrictive, thus the model becomes:

$$y_{it} = \alpha_0 + y_{i-1t} + \alpha_1 X_{1it} + \alpha_2 X_{2i} + \alpha_3 X_{2i} \cdot time + u_i + \rho_i \cdot time + \varepsilon_{it} \quad (C.2)$$

Differencing yields the model we estimate:

$$\Delta y_{it} = \alpha_1 \Delta X_{1it} + \alpha_3 X_{1it-1} + \rho_i + \Delta \varepsilon_{it} \quad (C.3)$$

Equation (C.3) will allow us to identify the effect of time-invariant factors on growth, while controlling for the changes in time-variant determinants of earnings levels. Moreover, when modeling growth from period t–1 to t, we can include time-variant factors measured at time t–1 among the time-invariant characteristics in X_{2i}. This approach, explained in Quinn and Teal (2008), is motivated by the observation that time-variant characteristics measured at t–1 that are predetermined are effectively time invariant with respect to growth between t–1 and t, and can therefore be included among the time-invariant regressors.

At the risk of belaboring the point, this equation allows discrimination between changes in earnings due to changes in explanatory variables-the "levels" effect of such variables-and changes due to the fact that explanatory variables might have an additional impact on individual earnings growth rates, the "growth" effects of such variables. To understand the difference, an analogy with the growth accounting literature may be of interest. Consider a steady state earnings growth trajectory, where earnings grow at a constant speed g and where individual and job characteristics are fixed such that $X_{1it} = X_{1it-1} = X_i^*$ then $g = \alpha_3 X_i^* + \rho_i$. In other words, the coefficient α_3 measures the effect of the variables X_i^* on the long-run growth path. By contrast, the coefficients α_1 only affect earnings growth during adjustment to the steady state equilibrium.

The above model can be estimated with OLS if we are willing to assume that the error term is uncorrelated with the explanatory variables, for example, if (OLS A1): $E[X_{1is}\varepsilon_{ij}] = 0 \ \forall \ s,t \ \varepsilon \{t, t{-}1\}$ and $E[X_{1is}\rho_i] = E[X_{2i}\rho_i] = 0 \ \forall \ s,t \ \varepsilon \{t, t{-}1\}$ (OLS A2). As in chapter 4, the fixed effect ρ can be tackled by using fixed effects and first-differences estimators.

Tackling Measurement Error: The Determinants of Earnings Growth over a Two-Year Period

The lack of strong predictors of earnings growth might partially be due to measurement error; if earnings are measured with a great deal of error, this may lead to attenuation bias. To overcome this problem, we estimated regressions where the growth of earnings over a two-year period is used as the dependent variable. The advantage of using a longer time window is that the signal-to-noise ratio in the data ought to be higher, in the sense that the proportion of the observed change in earnings that is due to measurement error should be smaller over a two-year period than over a one-year period. On the other hand, using earnings changes over a two-year period might exacerbate attrition bias. In addition, the differenced sample is much smaller, leading to less precise estimates.

The estimates are presented in table C.1—for the purpose of comparability, results using annual changes in monthly income as the dependent variable are also included. As can be seen by comparing the columns, the pattern of results does not change dramatically. However, comparison of these specifications with those presented in table 5.1 does suggest that attrition bias may be a problem.

Table C.1 Determinants of Two-Year Growth in Log Earnings

	Ghana		Tanzania	
	2 year	1 year	2 year	1 year
	Coef/SE	Coef/SE	Coef/SE	Coef/SE
Male	−0.074	−0.042	−0.627**	−0.352**
	(0.110)	(0.072)	(0.259)	(0.155)
L2.age	−0.002	−0.001	0.015	0.008
	(0.005)	(0.004)	(0.017)	(0.011)
Height (cm)	0.005	0.000	0.010	0.000
	(0.009)	(0.005)	(0.024)	(0.013)
Years in formal education	−0.031	−0.012	0.028	0.022
	(0.037)	(0.025)	(0.103)	(0.060)
(educ²)/100	0.003	0.001	−0.008	−0.004
	(0.003)	(0.002)	(0.007)	(0.004)
Math score	0.001	−0.001	−0.010	−0.005
	(0.002)	(0.001)	(0.010)	(0.006)
L2.apprenticeship completed	0.032	0.004	0.274	0.182
	(0.091)	(0.065)	(0.307)	(0.182)
L2.apprentice (currently)	−0.375	0.284		
	(0.757)	(0.248)		
Δ_2Ln (hours)	−0.101	−0.110	0.211	0.189
	(0.092)	(0.075)	(0.294)	(0.250)
Δ2tenure	−0.002	−0.002	0.024	0.024*
	(0.007)	(0.007)	(0.018)	(0.014)
L2.tenure	−0.005	−0.000	−0.028	−0.001
	(0.007)	(0.005)	(0.028)	(0.016)
Δ_2Ln (employees)	−0.010	0.018	−0.076	−0.672**
	(0.113)	(0.143)	(0.315)	(0.324)
L2.Ln (employees)	0.202	0.091	0.081	−0.568
	(0.167)	(0.090)	(0.351)	(0.455)
Δ_2Ln (firm size)	0.071**	0.053*	0.131**	0.164***
	(0.031)	(0.030)	(0.066)	(0.058)
L2.Ln (firm size)	0.003	−0.003	0.168	0.179**
	(0.030)	(0.021)	(0.112)	(0.074)
Self -> priv wage	−0.331	−0.148	−0.468	−0.363
	(0.281)	(0.159)	(0.415)	(0.251)
Self -> public	−0.937	0.222	1.411*	0.721**
	(2.473)	(1.156)	(0.748)	(0.302)
Priv wage -> priv wage	0.028	0.002	−0.103	−0.467**
	(0.133)	(0.085)	(0.421)	(0.232)
Priv wage -> self	0.412	0.194	−0.205	0.091
	(0.487)	(0.304)	(0.530)	(0.590)
Priv wage -> public	0.288	−0.237*	0.448	−0.149
	(0.400)	(0.137)	(0.908)	(0.401)
Public -> public	0.051	0.018	0.514	−0.305
	(0.196)	(0.098)	(0.616)	(0.354)

table continues next page

Table C.1 Determinants of Two-Year Growth in Log Earnings *(continued)*

	Ghana		Tanzania	
	2 year	1 year	2 year	1 year
	Coef/SE	Coef/SE	Coef/SE	Coef/SE
Public -> self	−0.202	−0.007		
	(0.466)	(0.434)		
Public -> priv wage	−0.123	−0.067	−0.278	−0.615
	(0.242)	(0.148)	(0.735)	(0.412)
Constant	−1.281	−0.031	−0.757	0.652
	(1.491)	(0.848)	(3.595)	(2.052)
Number of observations	706	706	157	157
R^2	0.061	0.067	0.206	0.243
Adjusted R^2	0.022	0.028	0.047	0.092

Source: World Bank; values arrived at using the Tanzanian and Ghanaian UPSs.
Note: Coef = coefficient; SE = standard error.
***p<0.01   **p<0.05   *p<0.1

Controlling for Fixed Effects

To control for bias arising from unobserved time-invariant, individual-specific effects that impact growth and are also correlated with earnings, we estimate the preferred model by means of fixed effects and first differences estimators. Variables measuring the impact of doing an apprenticeship are removed since there are too few observations to draw reliable conclusions. The results of these regressions are presented in table C.2. Overall, the results do not change substantially, save for the estimated sectoral premia. The results of these specifications ought to be interpreted with caution, however, because the number of observations is relatively small.

Table C.2 FE and FD Estimates of Annual Earnings Growth

	Ghana		Tanzania	
	FD	FE	FD	FE
Method	Coef/SE	Coef/SE	Coef/SE	Coef/SE
lrearn				
l.Δage	0.228	0.186	0.102	0.102
	(0.362)	(0.435)	(0.070)	(0.137)
Δ_2Ln (hours)	−0.095	−0.053	0.160	0.160
	(0.090)	(0.107)	(0.223)	(0.438)
$\Delta_2$tenure	−0.009	−0.003	0.039	0.039
	(0.010)	(0.011)	(0.025)	(0.049)
Δtenure	−0.009	−0.002	0.035	0.035
	(0.011)	(0.009)	(0.029)	(0.057)

table continues next page

Table C.2 FE and FD Estimates of Annual Earnings Growth *(continued)*

	Ghana		Tanzania	
	FD	*FE*	*FD*	*FE*
Method	*Coef/SE*	*Coef/SE*	*Coef/SE*	*Coef/SE*
Δ_2Ln (employees)	−0.232	−0.019	−0.124	−0.124
	(0.178)	(0.165)	(0.517)	(1.012)
LΔLn (employees)	−0.450*	−0.146	−0.393	−0.393
	(0.265)	(0.215)	(0.639)	(1.253)
Δ_2Ln (firm size)	0.097***	0.069	0.069	0.069
	(0.038)	(0.045)	(0.092)	(0.181)
LΔLn (firm size)	0.077	0.041	−0.076	−0.076
	(0.054)	(0.057)	(0.199)	(0.390)
Δself->priv wage	−0.384	−0.250	−0.445	−0.445
	(0.269)	(0.319)	(0.407)	(0.796)
Δself->public	0.013	0.403	1.186	1.186
	(1.310)	(1.509)	(0.767)	(1.503)
Δpriv wage->priv wage	−0.989***	−0.540*	−1.954***	−1.954
	(0.302)	(0.300)	(0.744)	(1.458)
Δpriv wage->self	0.963**	0.627	1.131**	1.131
	(0.403)	(0.447)	(0.549)	(1.075)
Δpriv wage->public	−0.085	0.022	1.133*	1.133
	(0.378)	(0.408)	(0.597)	(1.170)
Δpublic->public	−1.117**	−0.547	−0.316	−0.316
	(0.484)	(0.374)	(0.701)	(1.374)
Δpublic->self	0.237	−0.114		
	(0.544)	(0.463)		
Δpublic->priv wage	−0.068	−0.197	0.047	0.047
	(0.244)	(0.248)	(0.589)	(1.155)
Year dummies	Yes	Yes	Yes	Yes
Constant	−0.252	−5.919	−0.242	−3.484
	(0.371)	(14.663)	(0.156)	(5.248)
Number of observations	706	1,461	157	602
R^2	0.070	0.059	0.107	0.113

Source: World Bank; values arrived at using the Tanzanian and Ghanaian UPSs.
Note: Coef = coefficient; SE = standard error; FD = first difference; FE = fixed effect.
***p<0.01   **p<0.05   *p<0.1

A Framework for Analyzing Transitions between Low- and High-Paid Employment

Econometric Framework

The model for low-pay/high-pay transitions is a first-order Markov model that accounts for the initial conditions problem and nonrandom retention by treating them as issues of multiple endogenous selection. The modeling framework is an adaptation of the model proposed by Cappellari and Jenkins (2004). More specifically, we use multivariate probit models to model low-earnings transitions between two consecutive years, pooling observations across observed transitions.

There are three parts to the most general model. The first equation models initial low-pay determination at $t–1$ to control for the initial conditions problem.

$$L_{it-1}^* = \beta X_{it-1} + u_{it-1} \text{ where } u_{it-1} = \mu_i + \delta_{it-1} \text{ and } L_{it-1} = I(L_{it-1}^* \geq \tau) \quad (D.1)$$

where X_{it-1} is a vector observable characteristic and u_{it-1} is an error term that is the sum of an individual-specific effect and white noise δ_{it-1}, and L_{it-1} is an indicator variable indicating whether individual i's earnings fell below the low-pay threshold in period $t–1$ or not.

The second equation models the probability that individuals whose earnings were observed at time $t–1$ will also be observed at time t, thus allowing for the possibility that individuals either exit the sample at t or become nonparticipants without earnings.[1]

$$R_{it}^* = \psi W_{it-1} + \varepsilon_{it} \text{ where } \varepsilon_{it} = \tau_i + \zeta_{it} \text{ and } R_{it} = I(R_{it}^* \geq 0) \quad (D.2)$$

where W_{it-1} is a vector of observable characteristics that affect the retention propensity and ε_{it} is again an error term that is assumed to be composed of an individual-specific effect τ_i and white noise ζ_{it}. If individual i's retention probability is lower than a critical threshold, then his/her earnings are not observed in period t. R_{it} is an indicator variable that indicates whether an individual was retained.

The transition equation models low pay in period t, conditioning on low-pay status at $t-1$ as a function of observable characteristics X_{it}.

$$L_{it}^* = \left[L_{it-1}\gamma_1 + \left(1 - L_{it-1}\right)\gamma_2 \right] Z_{it-1} + v_{it} \text{ where } v_{it} = o_i + \pi_{it}$$

$$\text{and } L_{it} = I(\ L_{it}^* \geq \tau) \tag{D.3}$$

This specification is an endogenous switching regression, since the impact of covariates Z_{it-1} depends on the previous pay state. Again, the error process v_{it} is assumed to be composed of an individual-specific component and a random error process.

The error terms from the three equations are assumed normally jointly distributed, which implies a trivariate normal model that can be estimated using simulated maximum likelihood.

Allowing correlation between the three equations helps control for possible individual unobserved heterogeneity influencing both initial likelihood of low pay and transition between pay states, and hence to explore whether unobserved differences account for persistence in low earnings.

Likelihood Function

The truncated trivariate probit model to account for endogeneity due to nonretention has the following likelihood function:

$$InL = \sum_{i=1}^{N} R_{it} \Phi_3 \left(k_{i1} \left[L_{it-1}\gamma_1 + \left(1 - L_{it-1}\right)\gamma_2 \right] Z_{it-1}, \ k_{i0}\beta X_{it-1}, k_{iR}\psi W_{it-1}, \ \rho_1, \ \rho_2, \rho_3 \right)$$

$$\tag{D.4}$$

$$+ (1 - R_{it})\Phi_2 (k_{i0}\gamma Z_{it-1}, k_{iR}\psi w_{it})$$

where $k_{i1} = 2L_{it} - 1$, $k_{i0} = 2L_{it-1} - 1$, and $k_{iR} = 2R_{it} - 1$.

This model can be computed using maximum simulated likelihood (Cappellari and Jenkins 2003; Train 2003). As observed above, we pool transitions across multiple years. To correct for potential violations of the assumption that errors are identically and independently distributed, standard errors are clustered.

It should be noted that the normality assumption is violated by construction due to the presence of a lagged dependent variable in the transition equation and that same lagged dependent variable being one of the equations estimated. However, the normality assumption is required for tractability. Furthermore, Cappellari and Jenkins (2004) argue that violations of this assumption do not significantly affect the results.

Model Specification-Bivariate Models

While this framework allows the model to control for the initial conditions and nonrandom retention, below we present bivariate models of earnings transitions that control for the initial conditions problem only. The bivariate models use personal characteristics (education, gender, age, height, whether the person has ever been an apprentice) and job characteristics (sector dummies, tenure, firm size, or number of employees) as well as dummies for current city and survey year as explanatory variables. Parental education is used as an instrument for the initial conditions equation. Table D.1 shows the model specification tests for the bivariate models in both countries. Parental education instruments function well; we cannot reject that they are insignificant in the transition equation, but do strongly reject that they are insignificant in the initial low earnings equation. The estimated correlation between unobservables in the two equations is negative in both countries, though insignificant in Tanzania, which could reflect that, because of a smaller sample size in Tanzania, the true correlation in the population could not be uncovered. This also suggests that there is "regression to the mean" in the sense that individuals who were low paid last year are more likely to be high paid this year, potentially reflecting an error in the earnings measurement.

Transition Probabilities

Both the bivariate and trivariate models allow calculation of the low-income persistence rate s_{it} (the probability of being low paid at t, conditional on being low paid at $t-1$) and the low-income entry rate e_{it} (the probability of being low paid at t, conditional on being high paid at $t-1$).

$$s_{it} \equiv \Pr(L_{it} = 1 | L_{it-1} = 1) = \frac{\Phi_2\left(\gamma_1` Z_{it-1}, \beta`x_{it-1}; \rho\right)}{\Phi(\beta` x_{it-1})} \tag{D.5}$$

$$e_{it} \equiv \Pr(L_{it} = 1 | L_{it-1} = 0) = \frac{\Phi_2\left(\gamma_2` Z_{it-1}, -\beta`x_{it-1}; -\rho\right)}{\Phi(-\beta` x_{it-1})} \tag{D.6}$$

Table D.1 Bivariate Specification Tests in Tanzania and Ghana

	Test	Test statistic	P value
Ghana	Exclusion of parental education from transition equation	0.09	0.95
	Exclusion of parental education from initial equation	12.75	0.00
	Rho = 0	−2.13	0.033
	No state dependence	370.46	0.00
Tanzania	Exclusion of parental education from transition equation	0.79	0.67
	Exclusion of parental education from initial equation	15.99	0.00
	Rho = 0	−1.58	0.11
	No state dependence	97.82	0.00

Source: World Bank; values arrived at using the Tanzanian and Ghanaian UPSs.

The numerators in (D.5) and (D.6) are the probability that L_{it} is 1 or 0, respectively, at time t, given period t–1 characteristics, with Φ_2 being a bivariate normal cumulative density function and ρ measuring the correlation between the transition equation (equation D.3 above) and the initial low-pay equation (equation D.1). These probabilities are conditioned on either being low paid or high paid at t–1, being either 1 or 0, hence these events appear in the denominator in each equation, Φ being a univariate normal cumulative density function.[2]

The endogenous switching model implies regressors have different effects, depending on whether conditioning on high or low pay. Hence, the main analysis explores the effects of regressors both on s_{it} and e_{it}. In addition, this analysis also examines what changes in covariates imply for predicted mean and median time in low and high pay. If it is additionally assumed to be a stationary environment, we can calculate mean and median duration of low and high pay: the formula for mean duration of low pay is $1/(1-s_{it})$ and for the median duration it is $\log(0.5)/\log(s_{it})$. For those in high pay, the mean duration of a spell of high pay is $1/e_{it}$ and the median duration is $\log(0.5)/\log(e_{it})$ (for proofs, see Boskin and Nold [1975]).

State Dependence

Aggregate state dependence (ASD) is defined here as the difference between the probability of being low paid at t for those low paid at t–1 and the probability of being low paid at t for those not low paid at t–1.

$$ASD = \left\{ \frac{\sum_{i \in \{L_{it}=1\}} \Pr(L_{it=1} \mid L_{it-1} = 1)}{\sum_i L_{it-1}} \right\} - \left\{ \frac{\sum_{i \in \{L_{it}=0\}} \Pr(L_{it=1} \mid L_{it-1} = 0)}{\sum_i (1 - L_{it-1})} \right\}$$

While measures of ASD are arguably less prone to measurement error than measures of raw state dependence, they do not control for individual heterogeneity. By contrast, genuine state dependence (GSD), defined as the average difference between the predicted probabilities of being low paid, conditional on being low paid and high paid, controls for both unobserved and observed characteristics.

$$GSD = \frac{1}{N} \sum_{i=1}^{N} \Pr(L_{it} = 1 \mid L_{it-1} = 1) - \Pr(L_{it} = 1 \mid L_{it-1} = 0)$$

GSD is thus the preferred measure of state dependence. If differences in observed individual characteristics are the main drivers of initial pay states and transitions between states, then one would expect GSD to be lower than ASD. If labor market scarring is occurring, then one would expect GSD to be greater than zero.

Results

Maximum Likelihood (ML) Coefficients from Underlying Model

Table D.2 shows coefficient estimates from the underlying maximum likelihood estimation of the bivariate models. The coefficient estimates for the other equations are available, but were omitted to conserve space. The first column shows the effects of covariates conditional on being high paid, the second is conditional on being low paid (both in the transition equation), and the third is the p value from a test of whether these effects are significantly different from each other. Coefficient estimates are generally not significant in the transition equation, mainly because we control for initial selection into low pay in a separate equation, where all the coefficients are highly significant. Hence, a more intuitive method of examining the effects of individual and job characteristics is to explore their effects on the predicted probabilities of persistence of low pay, s_{it}, and entry into low pay, e_{it}, also allowing these to affect the probability of being low paid in the base period (see chapter 6).

Trivariate Model

This study only shows results for the trivariate specification for Ghana (table D.3), since the smaller sample size in Tanzania led to estimates that were not robust across specifications and to models that did not always converge, given the higher dimension of numerical integration required. Table D.4 shows that in Ghana, the correlation coefficient between the initial earnings equation and the transition equation is negative and significant, as in the bivariate case, and the magnitude is also similar to the bivariate model estimated above. Table D.4 also shows that the correlation coefficient between the transition equation and retention equations is positive and significant, suggesting that unobserved characteristics that make an individual low paid in the next period also increase the probability of the survey obtaining an earnings measure in the next period. The instruments for selection into initial low earnings work, and results show that the instruments for retention are not significant in the transition equation.

Again, our analysis focuses on the effects of changing covariates on both persistence and entry probabilities, shown in Table D.5. The results seem to be robust across specifications, with almost all the estimated effects in the trivariate model for Ghana qualitatively the same as in the bivariate model. However, there is now less of a difference in the variance of entry and persistence rates than the bivariate model suggested. Compared to the reference individual, women are nearly twice as likely to enter low pay, and younger workers are again more likely to remain in or enter low pay. Older and more educated workers are less likely to enter low-paid employment in future periods.

Table D.2 Maximum Likelihood Coefficient Estimates for Bivariate Probit

	Ghana			Tanzania		
	High earner	Low earner	P value coefficient equality	High earner	Low earner	P value coefficient equality
Male	−0.215**	0.215	0.077	−0.261	−0.138	0.774
	(0.106)	(0.152)		(0.213)	(0.294)	
Age	−0.004	0.007	0.351	0.008	−0.020	0.191
	(0.005)	(0.007)		(0.010)	(0.014)	
Years in formal education	−0.019	−0.006	0.846	0.201***	−0.118	0.050
	(0.034)	(0.047)		(0.075)	(0.101)	
(educ^2)/100	0.008	0.257	0.619	−1.944***	0.729	0.113
	(0.264)	(0.380)		(0.719)	(1.089)	
Priv wage	0.032	−0.308	0.358	0.056	0.364	0.745
	(0.157)	(0.225)		(0.427)	(0.580)	
Public	−0.187	0.550	0.135	−0.544	0.425	0.496
	(0.214)	(0.425)		(0.707)	(0.929)	
Tenure	0.008	−0.016*	0.107	−0.013	0.030*	0.127
	(0.006)	(0.010)		(0.014)	(0.018)	
Ln (hours)	0.152	0.003	0.479	−0.008	0.224	0.699
	(0.118)	(0.146)		(0.323)	(0.390)	
Ln (employees)	−0.170	0.385**	0.084	−0.307	0.638	0.131
	(0.128)	(0.185)		(0.300)	(0.428)	
Ln (firm size)	−0.049	0.204**	0.025	−0.117	0.233	0.199
	(0.048)	(0.082)		(0.127)	(0.208)	
Apprenticeship completed	−0.089	−0.005	0.696	−0.157	0.818*	0.173
	(0.099)	(0.130)		(0.311)	(0.438)	
Height (cm)	0.002	−0.003	0.718	0.002	−0.022	0.390
	(0.007)	(0.009)		(0.013)	(0.018)	
Number of observations			2,275			1,485

Source: World Bank; values arrived at using the Tanzanian and Ghanaian UPSs.
Note: ***$p<0.01$ **$p<0.05$ *$p<0.1$

Table D.3 Maximum Likelihood Coefficients for Trivariate Model, Ghana

	High earner	Low earner
Male	−0.221**	0.105
	(0.096)	(0.133)
Age	−0.004	0.003
	(0.005)	(0.007)
Formal education	−0.015	0.020
	(0.032)	(0.047)
(educ^2)/100	−0.079	−0.042
	(0.256)	(0.379)
Tenure	0.008	−0.017*
	(0.006)	(0.009)
Ln (hours)	0.172	−0.020
	(0.126)	(0.154)
Priv wage	−0.009	−0.254
	(0.152)	(0.216)
Public	−0.219	0.194
	(0.201)	(0.439)
Ln (employees)	−0.133	0.174
	(0.124)	(0.191)
Ln (firm size)	−0.028	0.166**
	(0.045)	(0.079)
Apprenticeship completed	−0.047	0.102
	(0.098)	(0.128)
Number of observations	2,932	2,932

Source: World Bank; values arrived at using the Tanzanian and Ghanaian UPSs.
Note: ***$p<0.01$ **$p<0.05$ *$p<0.1$

Table D.4 Trivariate Specification Tests for Ghana

	Test statistic	P value
Exclusion of parental education from transition equation	0.93	0.63
Exclusion of parental education from initial equation	12.75	0.00
$\rho1=\rho\_$transition/initial $=0$	−1.76	0.08
$\rho2=\rho\_$transition/retention$=0$	2.13	0.03
$\rho3=\rho\_$initial/retention$=0$	0.91	0.36
No state dependence	160.42	0

Source: World Bank; values arrived at using the Tanzanian and Ghanaian UPSs.

Table D.5 Predicted Entry and Persistence Rates and Mean and Median Predicted Time in Low Pay for Ghana, Trivariate Normal Model

	Low entry (%)	Mean high	Median high	Low persist (%)	Mean low	Median low
Reference	8.35	11.98	7.95	29.61	1.42	0.57
Education	5.63	17.77	11.97	23.94	1.31	0.48
Female	14.56	6.87	4.41	38.20	1.62	0.72
Small firm	7.42	13.48	8.99	27.79	1.38	0.54
Public employee	4.21	23.75	16.11	21.21	1.27	0.45
Age 40	7.17	13.94	9.31	27.24	1.37	0.53
Apprentice	8.23	12.15	8.07	33.64	1.51	0.64
Tenure	8.70	11.50	7.62	27.01	1.37	0.53
1 employee	6.38	15.68	10.52	28.18	1.39	0.55
Age 20	11.27	8.87	5.79	35.05	1.54	0.66

Source: World Bank; values arrived at using the Tanzanian and Ghanaian UPSs.

Notes: The reference person is a 30-year-old self-employed male with no employees, who has seven years of education, five years of tenure in his current job, and never been an apprentice. *Low entry* refers to the probability of being low paid in the next period conditional on being high paid currently. *Low persist* refers to the probability of continuing to be low paid in the next period.

Notes

1. Modeling these processes separately (using two probit models instead of one) proved impossible with the data.

2. This result also holds for the trivariate model, by the well-known result that the marginal distribution of an X dimensional normal distribution is an X–1 dimensional normal distribution.

Bibliography

Belzil, C., and J. Hansen. 2002. "Unobserved Ability and the Return to Schooling." *Econometrica, Journal of the Econometric Society* 70 (5): 2075–91.

Boskin, M., and F. Nold. 1975. "A Markov Model of Turnover in Aid to Families with Dependent Children." *Journal of Human Resources* 10: 476–81.

Cappellari, L. 2002. "Do the 'Working Poor' Stay Poor: An Analysis of Low Pay Transitions in Italy." *Oxford Bulletin of Economics and Statistics* 64 (2): 87–110.

Cappellari, L., and S. P. Jenkins. 2003. "Multivariate Probit Regression Using Simulated Maximum Likelihood." *Stata Journal* 3 (3): 278–94.

———. 2004. "Modeling Low Income Transitions." *Journal of Applied Econometrics* 19: 593-610.

Card, D. 2001. "Estimating the Return to Schooling: Progress on Some Persistent Econometric Problems." *Econometrica* 69 (5): 1127–60.

Chen, S., and M. Ravallion. 2008. "The Developing World Is Poorer Than We Thought, But No Less Successful in the Fight Against Poverty." Policy Research Working Paper No. 4703, World Bank, Washington, DC.

Deaton, A. 1997. *The Analysis of Household Surveys: A Microeconomic Approach to Development Policy.* Washington, DC: World Bank.

Fafchamps, M., and M. Söderbom. 2006."Wages and Labor Management in African Manufacturing." *Journal of Human Resources* 41 (2): 346–79.

Fafchamps, M., M. Söderbom, and N. Benhassine. 2009. "Job Sorting in African Labor Markets." *Journal of African Economies* 18: 824–68.

Fields, G. 2008. "A Review of the Literature on Earnings Dynamics in Developing Countries." Mimeo.

Fields, G., P. Cichello, S. Freije, M. Menendez, and D. Newhouse. 2003a. "For Richer or for Poorer? Evidence from Indonesia, South Africa, Spain, and Venezuela." *Journal of Economic Inequality* 1 (1): 67–99.

———. 2003b."Household Income Dynamics: A Four-Country Story." *Journal of Development Studies* 40 (2): 30–54.

Fox, L., and M. Gaal. 2008. *Working Out of Poverty: Job Creation and the Quality of Growth in Africa.* Washington, DC: World Bank.

Heckman, J. 1981a. "Heterogeneity and State Dependence." In *Studies in Labor Markets*, edited by S. Rosen, 91-140. Chicago: University of Chicago Press Books.

———. 1981b. "The Incidental Parameters Problem and the Problem: Initial Conditions in Estimating a Discrete Time-Discrete Data Stochastic Process." In *Structural*

Analysis of Discrete Data with Econometric Applications, edited by C. Manski and D. McFadden, 114–17. London: MIT Press.

ILO (International Labour Organization). 2002. *Women and Men in the Informal Economy: A Statistical Picture*. Geneva: ILO.

Johansson de Silva, S., and P. Paci. *Beyond Job Creation: The Challenges of Developing an Employment Agenda in Developing Countrie. mimeo.*

Kahyarara, G., and F. Teal. 2008. "The Returns to Vocational Training and Academic Education: Evidence from Tanzania." *World Development* 36 (11): 2223–42.

Kingdon, G., J. Sandefur, and F. Teal. 2005. "Patterns of Labor Demand in Africa: Africa Region Employment Issues-Regional Stocktaking Review." Mimeo.

Maloney, W. 1999. "Does Informality Imply Segmentation in Urban Labor Markets? Evidence from Sectoral Transitions in Mexico." *World Bank Economic Review* 13 (2): 275–302.

Mead, D., and C. Liedholm. 1998. "The Dynamics of Micro and Small Enterprises in Developing Countries." *World Development* 26 (1): 61–74.

Moffitt, R., J. Fitzgerald, and P. Gottschalk. 1999. "Sample Attrition in Panel Data: The Role of Selection on Observables." *Annales d'Economie et de Statistique* 55 (56): 129–52.

Nickell S. 1981. "Biases in Dynamic Models with Fixed Effects." *Econometrica* 49 (6): 1417–26.

Pissarides, C. A. 2002. "Human Capital and Growth: A Synthesis Report." Technical Report 168, OECD Development Centre, Paris.

Quinn, S., and F. Teal. 2008. "Private Sector Development and Income Dynamics: A Panel Study of the Tanzanian Labour Market." Working Paper 2008–09, Centre for the Study of African Economies, University of Oxford, Oxford, UK.

Rankin, N., J. Sandefur, and F. Teal. 2007. "Learning and Earning in Africa: Why It Pays to Go to School." Mimeo, CSAE, Department of Economics, University of Oxford, Oxford, UK, June.

Söderbom, M., F. Teal, A. Wambugu, and G. Kahyarara. 2006. "The Dynamics of Returns to Education in Kenyan and Tanzanian Manufacturing." *Oxford Bulletin of Economics and Statistics* 68 (3): 261–88.

Stewart, M., and J. Swaffield. 1999. "Low Pay Dynamics and Transition Probabilities." *Economica* 66: 23–42.

Train, K. 2003. *Discrete Choice Methods with Simulation*. Cambridge, UK: Cambridge University Press.

Wooldridge, J. 2007. *Econometric Analysis of Cross Section and Panel Data*. Cambridge, MA: MIT Press.

Environmental Benefits Statement

The World Bank is committed to reducing its environmental footprint. In support of this commitment, the Publishing and Knowledge Division leverages electronic publishing options and print-on-demand technology, which is located in regional hubs worldwide. Together, these initiatives enable print runs to be lowered and shipping distances decreased, resulting in reduced paper consumption, chemical use, greenhouse gas emissions, and waste.

The Publishing and Knowledge Division follows the recommended standards for paper use set by the Green Press Initiative. Whenever possible, books are printed on 50 percent to 100 percent postconsumer recycled paper, and at least 50 percent of the fiber in our book paper is either unbleached or bleached using Totally Chlorine Free (TCF), Processed Chlorine Free (PCF), or Enhanced Elemental Chlorine Free (EECF) processes.

More information about the Bank's environmental philosophy can be found at http://crinfo.worldbank.org/wbcrinfo/node/4.

green press INITIATIVE